The Forward Book of Poetry

2018

This anthology was designed and produced by Bookmark, sponsor of the Prizes. Bookmark is a global content and communications company based in London, Toronto, Montreal, Santiago, Lima, New York, LA, Shanghai and Singapore. Bookmark uses consumer insights to develop measurable marketing strategies and creative propositions to engage consumers, drive sales, and transform brands. Clients include Patek Philippe, Air Canada, LATAM, Bombardier, Fairmont Hotels & Resorts, Explora, Standard Life, Tesco, American Express Travel, Mercedes-Benz, Christie's, Lindt, the Academy of St Martin in the Fields and StreetSmart. bookmarkcontent.com @bookmarkcontent

The Forward Book of Poetry
2018

LONDON

First published in Great Britain by
Bookmark · 83 Clerkenwell Road · London ECIR 5AR
in association with
Faber & Faber · Bloomsbury House · 74-77 Great Russell Street
London WC1B 3DA

ISBN 978 0 571 34077 4 (paperback)

Printed and bound by CPI Group (UK) · Croydon CR0 4YY

A CIP catalogue reference for this book
is available at the British Library.

To Ed Victor, in memoriam

Contents

Highly Commended Poems 2017

Foreword

None of us was shamefaced. Prizes and rankings have become an essential mechanism for promoting quality in many art forms and professions – everything from quantity surveying to Highland dancing. Why should poetry be any different?

As judges of the twenty-sixth Forward Prizes for Poetry, our experience obliged us to rub noses with poets we didn't know sufficiently well, or at all; and it introduced extraordinary new talents we might otherwise not have come across; and that is, in the end, the point of the exercise.

All that said, I don't think any of us felt anything other than queasy and clammy-palmed at having to reject so many wonderful poems and collections as we worked our way through the shortlist to the final winners. We hope this book corrects some of the inevitable injustices involved in any contest in which apples and pineapples, clams and quinces, are meticulously weighed and compared. Nobody made it to the shortlist that the judges didn't adore; but individually, and as a group, we regretted the absence of personal favourites and wonderfully talented writers, as piles of books accumulated, or shrank, on kitchen tables.

Reading so many collections of poems over a relatively short period gives one an intense and useful overview of the condition of poetry in English now. What struck us all was the range of technical virtuosity and verbal ingenuity in contemporary poetry. We had a real sense of a restless language breaking its own borders, still interrogating itself, still seethingly alive. We were presented with poems of immense rhythmic and syntactical complexity; poems in the guise of epigrams and essays; and profoundly traditional work, which seemed to demand the bated breath of a live audience. The influence of the 'greats' of past generations was strikingly clear, from the vivid shadow of Derek Walcott over new Caribbean writers, to echoes of Eliot, Heaney and Yeats. Only books published in the UK and Ireland are eligible for the Forwards, but the English language – and new literature in English – is both global and local: excellent writing came in from every part of the world.

In terms of theme, we were confronted by contemporary politics, including the Brexit controversy and raw issues of race and immigration. We found poetry operating almost as a kind of higher journalism, snapshot reports from the dangerous borderlines of our world and some pessimistic writing about the condition of modern Britain, from northern railway stations to the streets of London.

But if there's a single common subject emerging from our reading, then it is a revival of the religious and the numinous, an enthusiasm for grappling with worlds and meanings beyond the physical. This spiritual appetite ranged from the free-verse psalms of Maria Apichella, in which a Christian anatomizes her love affair with an atheist; to the myth-haunted Caribbean world of Richard Georges; and the urban, ambitious epistemological questioning of Nuar Alsadir. Emily Berry, towards the beginning of her career, entangles herself in the grief of bereavement 'at the dangerous shore' while Michael Longley, towards the end of his, reflects in poems of beautiful, limpid simplicity on survival and resurrection.

There are, collected here, some poems that are difficult, requiring re-reading and concentrated thought; and others that can be embraced and enjoyed in a single scan. There are rude poems, cheeky poems, angry poems and poems of celebration.

Though an enthusiastic reader of poetry all my life, I had had no idea of the variety of the delights and provocations lying all around me.

This year, work by some very successful and famous poets didn't 'make the cut' but that was only because of the unavoidable quality of work by some less well-known people which did.

I came away more convinced than ever that if you read journalism alone, or history alone, or even add novels to those genres, and yet you omit contemporary poetry, then you cannot properly understand the world you live in.

I'd like to pay tribute to my fellow judges, the poet and critic Sandeep Parmar, the poets Mona Arshi and Ian Duhig, and the artist Chris Riddell. They flung themselves into a great deal of reading and thinking and note-taking for small reward beyond the reproachful glances of friends who didn't make it. They did the job for the love of the art form and they did it very well.

The world of poetry is both intensely political and feels itself hemmed in, surrounded by a sea of hostility and indifference. Yet charged, sharpened and rhythmic language has never been more important in what we are pleased to call our civilisation.

Those little, vividly coloured 'slim volumes', artfully designed to fit, but not quite, into a coat pocket, smoke with menace and sly humour. On the new landscapes of the internet, and in live events throughout the country, poetry continues to win new addicts.

I hope that, turning the pages ahead of you in this anthology, and turning some of them down to mark, and spending odd moments, day after day, with them, you will fall in love again with the most delicate and powerful of the arts.

Andrew Marr, *May 2017*

Preface

This anthology is a showcase, bringing together a selection of the best poetry published in the 12 months running up to September 2017. At the front you will find work by the 15 poets shortlisted for the three Forward Prizes – Best Collection, Best First Collection, Best Single Poem. The rest comprises 50 highly commended poems that caught the eye of the jury, after considering 186 collections and 212 single poems.

Poets from Ireland and the Caribbean are particularly well represented in this year's haul, alongside striking new voices from America and Africa. Subjects touched upon include exile, Ordnance Survey maps, psychoanalysis, sunken slave ships, bears, sexual ambiguity, Brexit and the effect of the Beatles on Nottingham teenagers in 1963. The wars in Vietnam and Uganda – history now – are seen from angles un-imagined by journalists at the time. The elegy count is high: lost parents and lost loves live on in highly charged language.

Michael Longley, at 77 one of the oldest poets in the book, says that 'poetry takes advantage of all the things that words do'. As a working definition, this is generous, and apt: you will find poems here that praise, mourn, exhort, question, enrage and amuse, plus several that do all of these and more, while posing as a paragraph of prose, or a list of observations. Do not be deceived by the apparent casualness with which these last seem to be written. In a poem, there is nothing truly random: every breath you take while reading these lines aloud will have been taken by the poet before you, testing the music of each line.

A reader with a moment to browse will find phrases here and there that snag the attention, demanding to be read again. Is it the pleasure of rolling sounds around the mouth that's so diverting? A pattern of black marks on a white page? Or the challenge thrown down by an expression that's familiar, but off-kilter? Whatever it may be, do not resist. This is not a book to be devoured in one sitting, nor should it be read against the clock. Turn down the corners of its pages, share poems you enjoy and use them as a source of inspiration: we know that earlier Forward books have inspired Forward-shortlisted poets in the past because several have told us so.

This year's 15 shortlistees, asked for their advice to young writers, were particularly helpful. The responses contained some classics of the genre, ranging from Nietzsche's 'Become the one you are' (offered by Nuar Alsadir) to Tom Pickard's 'ADVICE TO YOUNG POETS: moisturise' (quoted by Emily Berry). I am grateful to Longley, again, for reminding us that Edward Thomas once said, 'Anything, however small, may make a poem. Nothing, however great, is certain to.' My favourite, however, is from Ishion Hutchinson: 'Get a great anthology, study it with a well-pointed pencil until you have covered over all the pages.' If you use this book in that way, share the evidence via Facebook or Twitter @ForwardPrizes #ForwardPrizes: the business of encouraging high standards of poetry means fostering high standards of poetry appreciation too.

The judges responsible for this selection are poetry lovers; each came at their task from a different starting point. Sandeep Parmar, a scholar at Liverpool University, studies poems as well as writing them. Ian Duhig and Mona Arshi write poems for a living. And Andrew Marr and Chris Riddell, journalist and artist respectively, look to poems for fresh ways of experiencing the world. They addressed their task with dedication, care and scrupulous fairness: they deserve our warmest thanks.

Thank you, too, to Casey Jones, Chris Carus, Alex Courtley, Fay Gristwood, Lucy Coles and Simon Hobbs at Bookmark, as our main sponsor Forward Worldwide is now known. The Forward Prizes, first awarded 26 years ago with their support, are a tribute to Bookmark's investment in the imagination: their enlightened commitment has long set a benchmark for literature sponsorship. The consistency of their backing is matched only by the quality of the Bookmark teams' attention to detail: they work long hours to ensure this book does justice to the writers and publishers featured.

We are indebted to Arts Council England, to the estate of the late Felix Dennis – which backs the Felix Dennis Prize for Best First Collection – and to the Esmée Fairbairn Foundation and the Monument Trust. The trustees of the Forward Arts Foundation – Martin Thomas, Nigel Bennett, Joanna Mackle, Robyn Marsack, Jacob Sam-La Rose and Giles Spackman – have been great supports. Susannah Herbert, the Foundation's executive director, works tirelessly on finding new ways of ensuring that the Prizes have an impact out of all proportion to their size: she has been helped in this by the great team at FMcM, led by Annabel Robinson and Fiona McMorrough.

Finally, huge thanks to Holly Hopkins, the Forward Prizes manager, who is responsible for all that happens behind the scenes, from calling books in to ensuring the awards ceremony goes smoothly. Her care and dedication are balanced by unfailing cheerfulness and courtesy: everyone involved in these awards, including the publishers and poets, is in her debt.

William Sieghart
Founder, Forward Prizes for Poetry
June 2017

Shortlisted Poems
The Forward Prize for Best Collection

Nuar Alsadir

Sketch 19

A woman in high heels walks slowly along the broken avenue. The boys tangle their leashes trying to get ahead, turn and look back at her, then veer up the hill towards the open field. The park can't contain their desire. It pours into the atmosphere in particles that speed and collide, cause small children to lose their balance and fall off their bikes. This is quantum entanglement on an unseasonably warm November afternoon, the smell of coffee from Bittersweet that makes me bend backwards into morning, the spring of another year, trip while rushing home to meet you—

Sketch 64

Pleasure and disgust, the border of desire, of aesthetics, where beauty and the uncanny meet—is this the brink one must always live on, bare and bear, the vulnerability necessitated in feeling alive? When I have bared myself, I feel a compulsion to send out a flurry of signals to adjust the reception of others, to scramble the image that may have been momentarily revealed of me—

Tara Bergin

The True Story of Eleanor Marx

I'm not going to tell you anything
That my psychoanalyst wouldn't tell you.
He too speaks in riddles.
He too proclaims we are all victims
Of our insurrections.
I will not stand up to him.

There are ten parts to the story…

The True Story of Eleanor Marx in Ten Parts

1.

Eleanor of the eight-hour day
Gets betrayed by Edward of the two faces.
She orders: chloroform, with just some traces
Of prussic acid – blue – a beautiful imitation.

2.

She says it's for the dog but she is the dog.

3.

The Housekeeper finds her dressed in white.
It's not her bridal dress, she's not a bride.
It's from her childhood. She lies as if asleep.
She has strangely purple cheeks.

4.

In her 'white muslin dress' she is laid out.

5.

The Coroner is exasperated with feeble Edward.
CORONER Was the deceased your wife?
EDWARD Legally?
CORONER Were you married to the deceased?
EDWARD Not legally.
CORONER What was her age?
EDWARD Forty.

(She was forty-three.)

6.
On Tuesday:
Fire –
But the Phoenix,
God of Suicide,
Doesn't rise.
And Edward doesn't claim her
Because now he has a real wife.

7.
So the urn that holds the ashes of the soft summer dress,
And of the woman who knew the power of the proletariat,
And of the chunk of poisoned apple that she bit under duress,
Is taken to the offices of the SDF.

8.
The offices are in Maiden Lane.

9.
And in the offices in Maiden Lane,
There is a cupboard with two glass panes.
And there they place her to remain
For years and years.
Her tears are dew
And she crushes nothing.

10.
Nearly all of this is true.

Emily Berry

Winter

When the new room was built my mother showed me What To Do In Case Of Fire. There were four metal rungs embedded in the balcony wall: this was the escape route. She did not show me (then) the other one.

What happened was, my mother was very very sad. She was so sad she could not hold up her head, she could not sit down, she could not lie down, she could not see out of the dark, my very sad mum.

In the course of my research I learned a new kind of love. This lesson taught me to pray. I made a prayer for my mother. By 'prayer' I mean a meditation on a want that can never be answered. A prayer for the dead alive inside the living. That's what it is to burn a flame. We were in the darkest days of winter, approaching the celebration of light.

I watched the white men in their pastel coats / Roll you up and put you away / They put you inside their white box / With its clicks and locks / And carried you far away

Aura

Listen to me   little water
I called you up   believing something
would arise   in me believing
I could make   you reappear
on my way   to the cemetery
every face was   luminous
as if they knew   something about
the dark   I think you
were in us all   reminding me not
to despair or if   despairing know
that we did not   lose each other
either side   of the calamity
we fused   you went inside
& I could not   see you
but afterwards   afterwards
I could see   underwater I
could see in the dark   I could see
with my eyes closed I could see past
the shimmer that separates the living
& the dead I knew there was nothing
no separation   it was just
aura the most   remarkable
sadness &   if only I would
keep looking   I would see you

Michael Longley

Angel Hill

Someone must be looking after the headstones.
It might be you with your easel and brushes
And your big sheets and charcoal for drawing
Snowdrop cumulus and lichen lettering.
Someone must be looking after the railings
And closing the rusty gate behind her.

Room to Rhyme

in memory of Seamus Heaney

I

I blew a kiss across the stage to you
When we read our poems in Lisdoonvarna
Two weeks before you died. Arrayed in straw
The Armagh Rhymers turned up at the end.

II

In the middle of a field in Mourne country
Standing side by side, looking straight ahead
We peed against a fragment of stone wall,
St Patrick's windbreak, the rain's urinal.

III

On our pilgrimages around the North
In your muddy Volkswagen, we chanted
Great War songs: *Hush! Here comes a whizz-bang!*
We're here because we're here because we're…

IV

Smashed after *Room to Rhyme* in Cushendall
We waded through heather-stands to Fair Head
And signed our names in biro on Davy's shirt
And launched it off the cliff into the wind.

V

We drove after Bloody Sunday to join
The Newry March – road blocks, diversions –
Time enough to decide, if we were asked
At gunpoint: *And what religion are you?*

VI

When Oisin Ferran was burned to death, you
Stood helpless in the morgue and wept and wept.
Awaken from your loamy single-bed:
Kiss me on the lips in Lisdoonvarna.

Sinéad Morrissey

Perfume

I

23 May 1963

My Great Auntie Winnie may as well have spotted a crack
        in the floor of Nottingham's Odeon Cinema –
                beginning under the stage
like a telltale hairline fissure in a dam face
        then zigzagging towards the exit –
                as have been struck
by the actual bellwether that assailed her
        the morning she trudged in to sweep and mop
                and dust the flip-back seats
after the pop music concert the night before:
        not just the common-enough stench of smoke
                and sweat, but an extra still-warm
acrid musk, the mixed-in fug of a stable
        in summer heat, hitting her like the reek
                of a hospital laundry,
because in answer to *Love Me Do*, offered up
        in spectacular harmony, two hundred
                fourteen-year-old girls
had instantly wet themselves, screaming *Yes!*
        We love you already!, but inaudibly,
                each lone voice hopeless
against the squealing sheetmetal square of noise,
        and so their bodies had taken over,
                take this river, each shower a gift,
intimate and articulate, to whichever identikit member
        they'd pinned their collapsing
                stomachs on, each stream of steaming
yellow a flower, and as the crack grew ever wider
        and plaster flakes abandoned the ceiling

and covered my Auntie's rollered
hair, she suddenly saw the street outside
divide the length of the fissure, then the city,
the north, the south, then all of England,
mothers on one side, daughters on the other,
and the chasm between them strung
with brilliant washing –
socks and vests and stockings and skirts and pants,
rinsed clean with a bluebag in the kitchen sink,
lifting in the wind.

My Life According to You

So I was born and was small for ages
and then suddenly a cardboard box
appeared with two furry black ears
sticking out of it it made me nervous
but I was brave and gave it a bell
to play with and then out it jumped
and loved me it was my cat I called it
Morris Morrissey it matched
my mother's Morris Minor

For the next bit

I was a teenager and then I grew up
I had a flat in Dublin and a boyfriend
he was a vet little bed little kitchen
little towel rack lots of little cups
and saucers and then off he went
to Africa he sent me pictures
of giraffes and of the second
tallest waterfall in the world
when he got back he wasn't my friend

anymore I cried

for a week I was also at university
a bigger place than school with bigger
chairs and desks and when it finished
I found a suitcase it was red
with purple flowers it had a scarf
around the handle I put in everything
I needed socks and a jotter and snacks
and took a plane across the ocean
to Japan to visit Godzilla

where it was

summer and boiling hot and the people
all kept wind chimes to make it
cooler and rode bicycles to the shops
and at the same time held up umbrellas
though it wasn't even raining
and when I met a man in a bright
white classroom the darkest parts
of our eyes turned into swirls then question
marks then hearts so we got married

and went hippety

hoppety splat a mountain a lake
a desert we bought a house a tiny one
at first and then a massive one a baby
knocked at the door one night
but didn't come in and then another
baby came he cried a lot
we thought he had a tummy ache
we gave him a bath in a bucket
he was just lonely

for his sister

to come and keep him company
but you were still floating about
in space inside your bubble egg
it had accessories a switch
for going sideways a switch
for going upside down or faster
it was a cross between a sparkly green
and a sparkly silver the moon
was very annoying and then whenever

we'd all been bored

on our own for long enough down
you came on a path of lightning
to finish off the family you were born
on the living room floor at three
in the morning in front of the trampoline-
sofa and I heard them say *A Girl!*
and sat up straightaway we were both
pretty and I opened out my arms
and that's it really

                        When you grow up

I'm going to be *so* busy taking you
to the house shop waiting by the play-
ground gates to bring your children
swimming I won't be any different
I'll keep your room exactly as it is
for you to visit bric-a-brac collection
on the shelf the bed your father built
the letters of your name in neon
appearing on the ceiling

                              when it's time

Shortlisted Poems
The Felix Dennis Prize for
Best First Collection

Maria Apichella

28.

Today the turquoise view
swoops faster, swirls like lime juice in a cold glass,
the bay flashes, tumescent, a noon-time joy, steep to the side.
The early moon a pale slice in blue. Scent of manure and hay blow,
sheep wink, coastline trees like brown twiggy hair blowing sideways.
My David's a pebble of strength too bright,
too smooth to be flung.
Nothing's certain but changing landmarks, sifting coves.
We're aware of each other's breathing; the Mini's forced nearness,
the sun catching his knuckles, freckled wrist, silver watch,
his quiet shifting of the gears, dusty brown Topsiders stepping hard
on the gas   rising   high.
And down
            deep to the mossy,
            valley house. A white block
            windowed memory.
We click still.
A net curtain moves.

Before I meet his mother
he takes me
among his father's rocky fields,
shows me how to swindle
honey from a hive.
With a cigarette *just for this purpose*
he puffed acrid smoke like an old rusty engine.
A slow thrum,
the sound of tiny drills.
The conquered *Gwenynen Fêl*
shot up, away into the blue,
her drones chasing like a chorus of boy-lovers.
I had been hungry.
He gave me the first sticky comb.

58.

We meet my friends; 'church people,'
by which you mean:
'quiche eaters,
side-huggers,
hand-squeezers,
men who wear socks in bed.'

You analyse them across the linen covered table,
they consider you through candlelight.

Over custard and crumble we strayed
into talk of prayers. You snorted,
said it's like a child's bludgeoned knee
kissed better.
I stirred your meaning, squeezing
subtleties like lemon juice
over the peppery sounds of your hot tongue,
as if to say –

Richard Georges

Ghazal of Guyana

Do you see? The bones of stars are falling,
crashing to the earth like trees, like greyed spears

again I find myself amidst a frieze of bodies
lost in our commune of ritual sweat

a hurricane is spinning Saharan
winds through the constellation of islands

they whisper my name from the muddy rows
of cane, reminding me, *the flesh is sin*

the trees ache in the light, their ashen limbs
a warning to birds: *do not alight here*

this tree which is not a way of breathing
of keeping your head above whipping waves

we praise in spit and surf to our God
but not to this sea which is everything

until I can *not* help but think that I
am again: *a flesh and blood poetry*

my sister can remember how to make
baigan, blistering bulbs on splitting flames

on the Parika bank of the river
a boy sells water out of a rice sack

in my office sits a stoic Ganesh
intricately carved out of fiberglass.

Oceans

I once tried to hold the ocean
in my hands, in a glass

in the past, the sea
would grind the bones

of slaves, of sailors
into sand. Even the sand

can be lessened. Like us
when cold water pushes past

lips, teeth, tongue, throat,
into lungs, and all is filled cold.

The ocean is a universe.
An abyss consuming even light in its depth.

What word? What voice moving
over its dark currents?

In my glass, the ocean is radiant,
is effervescent, a mouth tracing the body.

I want to roll an ocean
into a ball in my hands.

I want to hold it up to my eye,
to search for imperfections I know are not there.

I map Africa. America.
Europe. Asia. Continents like

opposing parentheses enclosing nothing
except the histories of too many people.

A broken book of poems,
stanzas falling like shards.

Oceans slip out of me,
Middle Passage, Kala Pani.

I parted your legs and between them
I discover another ocean.

There is an ocean between us
I cannot cross like my ancestors did

And so we all remain. Divided.
Like the shores of islands.

I held an ocean in my mouth,
its cresting waves tickled my palate,

my tongue oared its waves
but I could go nowhere.

The ocean between us has
swallowed the ground, swallowed the sky,

and all of this is only water.

Eric Langley

1. Of those from the ships

'Ptolemaeus the king of Egypt was so eager to collect a library, that he ordered the books of everyone who sailed there to be brought to him. The books were then copied into new manuscripts. He gave the new copy to the owners ... but he put the original copy in the library with the inscription "of those from the ships."'

Galen

So you can come along and you can scan it:
come along the docks, as are your curious customs,
and you can move among my spread
among my freight my cargo.
And you should catch a draft to drift
to drift from crate my love to crate
my love through freight my lovely argosy.

So you can leaf your dusty tips through wheat and chaff
and riffle out each inky index
through all the silken slough
of all my gaudy textiles.
Flick through it, resort it, recall it
to recount and to your count enlist
my disembarked, my unencrypted holdings.

And so, ascribe each part, just so,
inscribe each piece, just so,
describe each Hippocrene flask, just so,
each cask, just so: of all my all content.
To each a place in place to place
in your exact accountant call
of row by rolling row anatomies.

Now as you go, steady
my dizzying inventories, steady

my whole to holed in hold and steady as you go.
Until amongst the richer sort, my finer stuff,
my love, my weft, my warp, my woof, my loom,
you come across, you chance upon
my books, my textured library.

Like Antony, enlisting scrolls for Egypt,
I've weighed up with ranks of primed romance,
rows of charged letters, waxed flattery.
Please read them quick; respond at length but
on the instant, as each squeezed line tips
tight up on the grazed edge, squeaks 'come!'
and soft speaking means the softly same.

Pinched, each plundered volume plumbs
your depths of cheek of face of front.
The bitter gall of it, from row to row
shelf to shelf and decimal point to point.
You and your low-toned underlings, *sotto voce*,
unstack, stack up, pack up and off
with those, all those from my ships.

Your tough customs, your officious vandals,
all horn-rimmed reading glasses
and hob-nailed boots spectacular
along my aisles, through my stacks,
and scrawling down my gangplanks.
So silence please. And no talk back to back
to no recourse to no redress to silence please.

You rogue librarian, filling packing cases;
you rough justice, packing shipping crates;
you vile bibliophile, stealing a borrow;
you unrepentant lovely lender.
Fingered, found red-handed
shameless-faced, each fly defaced:
of those – you wrote – *from the ships*.

You with their hollow whispers
of silenced, pleased apology
towing away my textures
of those from the ships
You book thieves pirates book robbers;
you book thieves collectors borrowers lovers
of those from the ships

Of course, I knew your Alexandrian law.
I knew you'd come, and knew you'd take them.
Of course, I brought along my best materials –
first editions, originals, manuscripts –
and must have hoped you'd steal them.
This is the hope, of course off course,
of all those from such a stricken ship

of all those from the ships.

Pentimenti

I.

So, trickster, there I am, tucked into the grass
for you to glance at behind flat glass.

So, saboteur, there we are, sunk knee-deep in the inch-thick,
fat to the gummy wooze, made up full in the facture

while each eye draws to the door, while every eaves-
dropper snugs chop-chop to the rafters.

We are at one jump, one kick beyond the ordinary.
We are at jump, *right to it*: fingers loved in the colour tone;

fists tight to the high thrum; limbs lain twist in the warp,
in, at the first weave

                      stitched   and oh-so starkly starkly
               without a dry thread on.

II.

I'm going further in among black orchids,
among black hyacinths, lurking in the opacity

of an overgrown orchard, snapping into our
interminable débris of revision

                        sinking
                            into the underdrawn.

You – soft between the dials and tentive to the redials –
slipped me soft off hook, switched clear off a clean step,

and left me lost out here – dialling, dialling – left me
out of each and every key exchange, to loop and loop

through each of every bad bad branchline's reach.
So wrung out rung in starkstruck reroute right round

such nerve-taut tough telephonics, O, such livewire centres,
O, such rough rate centres, such awesome plugboard din.

III.

And so, this should be seen as all wild-eyed in capped careen
unhushed, and come as a desperate dive, a last gasped finely final call

– falling galled appalled –
in dumb steamed crambo – as comeback come back please:

as
one for the road.

But this then stands around like a late careering, hit
against hope: a shot sliced askance to the fine grain; adrift

to the rainfall, just a doe-struck call-back reeling back,
back to the clumsy couch, to hot drops on the plastic roof –

just crude flesh and hipbone, back to rude things,
that mattered: raw things, lost.

IV.

What, so I'm grown so tonedeaf in ringdown? What,
so I'm so lost in switch, so lost so lost to the patchcord crossfire

that you slip the ringing cord, that you drop the rear cord
slot to the hot electric jack – and there, among sharp static,

this buzzbell and fedback feedback fuzz that I'm calling?
                                    Out in the wire world.

Your lips, step out of cinch, broke clinch, but I mouth around
                    for our lovely wordstuff.

Dialled right on up to the cool-blue booty. Keeled right up and up
            to your hot neon-tips, your hot fluorescent, that peels off

among these screeds, and ravelling ravelling under their radars,
                    off from their cold cut tenderhooks;

the one last peaky tentation cast off in-coming kiss-me-quick
raiders homing in, in stealthy for even such an even-chance

    of such a hot
                                    catch-up.

Nick Makoha

Prayers for Exiled Poets

> *'Were you to ask me where I've been...*
> *I would have to tell how dirt mottles rocks.*
> *How the river, running, runs out of itself.'*
> Pablo Neruda, 'There is No Forgetting (Sonata)'
> translated by Forrest Gander

Prayers no longer hold up these walls in my absence.
My own country rebukes me. I hold the world on my back.

Look for me in translation. In my own language you will go
    unanswered.
My Ugandan passports are a quiet place of ruin.

Where I come from, money is water slipping through their hands.
They eat what falls from the trees and turns the flesh to gin.

I am of the same fruit and close to extinction.
My only root is my father's name. Both of us removed from the
    soil.

In recent times, despite my deeds, you let me stay
no longer in bondage between earth and sky. No longer

do I hide in my own shadow. No longer waiting to stop waiting.
This rock becomes a sanctuary from which I can repair the ruins.

You have given me back my eyes.

At Gunpoint

My body is the protagonist watched by soldiers
in patrol cars. Roof down, the front windscreen
frames them. Amin's voice bleeds
from a radio wafting up into a window of sky.

The *Times* will report of people
being forced to volunteer to avoid
being a body hiding in a toilet
or a corpse folded on a table.

I have heard men say *We will serve you.*
Others will say he saved them,
and yet others will flee, by passage
out to a border that no longer exists.

I have only made it as far as the long grass,
virgin territories whose mountain plains
and tribal inhabitants are a garnish,
part of a failed colonial experiment.

Holding my breath, words are now shadows
walking me down a corridor of all the wrong things
that brought me here. In this cracked republic
I have made a film of my life and played myself.

A man can't but look into his own imagination
to solve the conflict of himself. *Should I have been
the doctor, or a poacher in the clearing, a mad man,
or shepherd boys minding their business?*

All soldiers must die – some by bullet, some by knife;
the sharpest cut is betrayal. Lips are their usual servants.
I do not want to know the whistle of a bullet in the air
or how it seeks blood to release the weight of the soul.

Ocean Vuong

Telemachus

Like any good son, I pull my father out
of the water, drag him by his hair

through white sand, his knuckles carving a trail
the waves rush in to erase. Because the city

beyond the shore is no longer
where we left it. Because the bombed

cathedral is now a cathedral
of trees. I kneel beside him to see how far

I might sink. *Do you know who I am,
Ba?* But the answer never comes. The answer

is the bullet hole in his back, brimming
with seawater. He is so still I think

he could be anyone's father, found
the way a green bottle might appear

at a boy's feet containing a year
he has never touched. I touch

his ears. No use. I turn him
over. To face it. The cathedral

in his sea-black eyes. The face
not mine – but one I will wear

to kiss all my lovers good-night:
the way I seal my father's lips

with my own & begin
the faithful work of drowning.

Notebook Fragments

A scar's width of warmth on a worn man's neck.
>That's all I wanted to be.

Sometimes I ask for too much just to feel my mouth overflow.

Discovery: My longest pubic hair is 1.2 inches.

Good or bad?

7:18 a.m. Kevin overdosed last night. His sister left a message.
>Couldn't listen to all of it. That makes three this year.

I promise to stop soon.

Spilled orange juice all over the table this morning. Sudden
>sunlight I couldn't wipe away.

All through the night my hands were daylight.

Woke at 1 a.m. and, for no reason, ran through Duffy's cornfield.
>Boxers only.

Corn was dry. I sounded like a fire,
>for no reason.

Grandma said *In the war they would grab a baby, a soldier at each*
>*ankle, and pull…Just like that.*

It's finally spring! Daffodils everywhere.
>Just like that.

There are over 13,000 unidentified body parts from the World
Trade Center being stored in an underground repository in
New York City.

Good or bad?

Shouldn't heaven be superheavy by now?

Maybe the rain is 'sweet' because it falls
      through so much of the world.

Even sweetness can scratch the throat, so stir the sugar well. – Grandma

4:37 a.m. How come depression makes me feel more alive?

Life is funny.

Note to self: If a guy tells you his favorite poet is Jack Kerouac,
      there's a very good chance he's a douchebag.

Note to self: If Orpheus were a woman I wouldn't be stuck
      down here.

Why do all my books leave me empty-handed?

In Vietnamese, the word for grenade is 'bom', from the French
      'pomme', meaning 'apple'.

Or was it American for 'bomb'?

Woke up screaming with no sound. The room filling with a bluish
      water called dawn. Went to kiss grandma on the forehead

just in case.

An American soldier fucked a Vietnamese farmgirl. Thus my
mother exists. Thus I exist. Thus no bombs = no family = no me.

Yikes.

9:47 a.m. Jerked off four times already. My arm kills.

Eggplant = cà pháo = 'grenade tomato'. Thus nourishment
        defined by extinction.

I met a man tonight. A high school English teacher
        from the next town. A small town. Maybe

I shouldn't have, but he had the hands
        of someone I used to know. Someone I was used to.

The way they formed brief churches
        over the table as he searched for the right words.

I met a man, not you. In his room the Bibles shook on the shelf
        from candlelight. His scrotum a bruised fruit. I kissed it

lightly, the way one might kiss a grenade
        before hurling it into the night's mouth.

Maybe the tongue is also a key.

Yikes.

I could eat you he said, brushing my cheek with his knuckles.

I think I love my mom very much.

Some grenades explode with a vision of white flowers.

Baby's breath blooming in a darkened sky, across
        my chest.

Maybe the tongue is also a pin.

I'm gonna lose it when Whitney Houston dies.

I met a man. I promise to stop.

A pillaged village is a fine example of perfect rhyme. He said that.

He was white. Or maybe, I was just beside myself, next to him.

Either way, I forgot his name by heart.

I wonder what it feels like to move at the speed of thirst – if it's
fast as lying on the kitchen floor with the lights off.

(Kristopher)

6:24 a.m. Greyhound station. One-way ticket to New York
City: $36.75.

6:57 a.m. I love you, mom.

When the prison guards burned his manuscripts, Nguyễn
Chí Thiện couldn't stop laughing – the 283 poems
already inside him.

I dreamed I walked barefoot all the way to your house in the
snow. Everything was the blue of smudged ink

and you were still alive. There was even a light the shade of
sunrise inside your window.

God must be a season, grandma said, looking out at the blizzard
drowning her garden.

My footsteps on the sidewalk were the smallest flights.

Dear god, if you *are* a season, let it be the one I passed through
to get here.

Here. That's all I wanted to be.

I promise.

Shortlisted Poems
The Forward Prize for Best Single Poem

Malika Booker

Nine Nights

The Set Up

If you did see people that first night. People for so. Who come
from town, from far like St David, from near like St Mark to
this little St John parish. It had the makings of a good funeral.
Pure bus park up by Gouyave roadside like ants. Them mourners
arrived, shuffling with the shock. The priest opened up that wake
with plenty prayers. Corn soup bubbled in the iron pot, red beans
slowly converged with rice, thyme and coconut milk. Chairs
clustered like fowls in the yard. Till he mother fell down under the
weight of her dead son. *So young* she muttered *so young*.

Song

Grief song is a different story. A clap of hands then a rocking back
and forth story. Grief song is a body dancing to a jagged melody
story. Grief song is so searing, it's the belly drops to knees story.
Grief song is the way his mother sinks into the arms of *Rock of Ages*
story. I tell you Grief song is a hard to tell story.

The Dreams

Martha had dreams for so since the night he dead. And wise
woman Clarise could not make head nor tail of flying fish and
hummingbirds over rough river water. Of eddo swelling under
rocky soil. Of septic tank full of bleach and blue soap. *What does it
mean* she muttered *what does it mean?*

Funeral Announcement

To hear his name called dry so on radio – *was the son of… brother of… left behind* – bruck her up. And them doltish dogs howling a relentless dirge for they master who never pelt them with kick, who boil one fresh pot of dog food; chicken neck with gravy and white rice, every morning like greeting. Them dogs howl so till grief lock off they windpipe.

His Resurrection

When Lazarus fas up and step cross the threshold of he own wake, rank with corpse stink, the wake bruck up. Who put foot out of door quick time. Who start pray fast fast. Who faint and get revive with smelling salts. Miss Gibbs forget she hips bad, till she tek two steps and fall Bra-tap. Mr Power start moan bout the good good money he dash way on pretty funeral frock for Betty and now she can't even use it. Uncle Johnny start fling rum shouting *You   dead   man, you   dead!* like libation have any power over the resurrected.

Vexation

It had the makings of a boss funeral, mourners muttered, sulking into wake's shadow. Martha steups over and over like chant, her venomous kiss teeth terrifying even tough back crapo. Mary vex too bad, *How he could go and make their serious work of grief into a pappy show*. Mary head get hot – Look how much white candle he mother burn to light he way and how like stubborn jackass he refuse to follow instruction, *Just turn away from the light boldface so*. This was just like when he was hard ears to leave he mother womb. The old choir women in the back room stop singing and only cussing bad word, wild at the shame and slander of this thing.

Fling Down Party

Lazarus dash way hymns and cuss words from he house with the heavy bass of a thumping speaker box. The floor boards start tremble, as he foot rise up and skip, as he fingers lick and clap, when the Rasta man chant take over. *Give thanks*. Lazarus dance fire and brimstone. Dance chant down Babylon. Start lick fist on fragile board wall. Start shout *more fire, more fire* as if alive scatter springs into he steps; as if alive shake up he mind. He locs swinging like thick twine tied to air and he chanting *i&i livity, i&i livity*.

Geography of Resurrection

And when that reporter woman ask Lazarus *what it was like*, as they sat in the cream-wall room with the hum of mosquitoes and he say, *there is a chart to being resurrected. An atlas that have mud swamp, sweet water river and thorny paths. There is a one foot in front of another chart. A believe and it shall be chart. A surrender chart. A rhythm chant chart. And you just have to trod it all rude girl, you just have to trod it.*

The Laying of the Hands

And when they saw he still lived to this ninth day, they cancelled La Qua funeral parlour, grab he up in a white sheet, tote him swinging like he in a rocking hammock to the sea shore and roll him in the coarse hot sand. Then dunk he head in the salty sea, washing death's stench off of him. Then they anointed him – all palms seeking to touch their feeble miracle.

Mary Jean Chan

//

My mother lays the table with chopsticks & ceramic
spoons, expects you to fail at dinner. To the Chinese,

you and I are chopsticks: lovers with the same anatomies.
My mother tells you that *chopsticks* in Cantonese sounds

like *the swift arrival of sons.* My mother tongue rejoices
in its dumbness before you as expletives detonate: *[two*

women] [two men] [disgrace]. Tonight, I forget I am
bilingual. I lose my voice in your mouth, kiss till blood

comes so *sorry* does not slip on an avalanche of syllables
into sorrow. I tell you that as long as we hold each other,

no apology will be enough. Tonight, I am dreaming again
of tomorrow: another chance to eat at the feast of the living

with chopsticks balanced across the bridges of our hands
as we imbibe each *yes*, spit out every *no* among scraps of

shell or bone. Father says: *kids these days are not as tough
as we used to be. So many suicides in one week.* How many

times have you and I wondered about leaving our bodies
behind, the way many of us have already left? My friend's

sister loved a woman for ten years and each word she says
to her mother stings like a papercut. Each word she does

not say burns like the lines she etches carefully into skin.
I have stopped believing that secrets are a beautiful way

to die. You came home with me for three hundred days –
to show my family that dinner together won't kill us all.

Harmony Holiday

The City Admits no Wrongdoing

Somebody put a golden girlchild on a southern railway in the 1920s, with a satchel of chicken. Picnic for one. Northward toward a better life. Billie Holiday loved somebody who put her on a railway with a satchel of chicken. When the food ran out, they called them honkeys. The white men who drove up to Harlem in fancy lawn vehicles and honked outside of the houses of the goldenchild, praying for sex and no wrongdoing. O'Hara loved you. Orson Welles loved you. Miles loved you. You are loved. I love you, too, What is a heroin addiction, really? What does it indicate? What is the difference between a honkey and rapist? Can she live. Can the stage be riddens enough, the begged for bruises, the softly-spoken desire for a frozen pit bull and a club of her own, northern promise enough to make trouble up. Poised suffering. All she had to do was sing, one man wrote. And cook her dope into the chicken. God Bless the Child. The white actress Judy Garland was sent back to the country to wean off of heroin around the same time Billie Holiday was hospitalized, handcuffed to the bed, with no friends allowed to visit and her last five dollars strapped to her garter, and no candies. She loved candies. We need sugar. We run on sugar. Melanin is carbon. Carbon is sugar. Billie is shook, hurry, you love her. You worship the one you've broken. You still cook the fur off, chicken. *Sugar, I call my baby my sugar, I never maybe my sugar, that sugar baby of mine. Funny, he never asks for my money…* Put on these amber glasses and all the light ain't blue.

Ishion Hutchinson

Nightfall, Jane Ash Corner, St. Thomas

Ice splits those millennia of canes.
They stand by the coppice
in ready patience and danger
when I pass by the barracks. A mongrel
pack, in their heat, vanishes
into a lane. Cane and silence.

Ash-frosts glimmer houses
sleeping by the factory.
I pause to breathe deep the molasses vat.
Progress is back, but centuries
are one here. Flogging
laughter in the schoolyard;

a book tortures ants, then gets
thrown into the latrine.
I hide blue bibles in tree roots,
until evenings, to take them home.
One lumps in my back pocket now; the embossed Gideon
and amphora I have not broken.

I am eyes in the old slave quarters.
The future will arrive in four years and burn
the river grouse green and kill
the library cormorant, whom
I had fallen for.
It will close the bible age.

Morning exhales pitch dark
on Peacock Hill. The rigid lines of tractors
hitched with hostel-size carts

come clear and the first cane cutters walking towards them
in burlap ponchos, most smaller
than me, or so it seems, leap over the errant-fish cistern.

Ian Patterson

The Plenty of Nothing

i.m. Jenny Diski, 1947–2016

Pale duty stamps about in plenty of nothing
    like the night when you know everything to time
when each step is beaten off when the rack might add
    more glory and I would watch the stars
not kin nor proof to rule the sphere to know
    by clothes and tea how to cut lino out of them

Now see who has the little boat of love and wave
    adrift more salt at its best splash scornful enough
away on your right to curve well in some hope then
    plunging like blame, my hat tossed up and bent
and lost wires lurid if there ever was one at hand
    to walk with me out of my mind's eye always apt

Old china caught to seize as springless nature seeps up
    and wells at stake to risk another fire
in a forest of beasts where silent stories end in a beer
    or in dark lists above the clause that starts to die
left to review by me my kindest cut scabbed as a free
    local disguise made naked to suffer for doing just that

You can give it up for hope's always a bit of web to ignore
    sound into the relief fire bad as you wish for
this lack of a figure in the grip of method on the screen
    to burst out of acid to be like last at the spindle instant
as a gripping vertigo flash vacuum leaves spores in place
    of humanism for us when this frolic unveils payment

End tricky time to get enough pink forms to reconcile
    two worlds of the mind to say the least at work
safe hands on what we know to move abroad like autumn

leaves the trees revealed at last as a mouthpiece for language
a copy to taste such stress detail at times of less art chat tangled
to a dead tune in sharp clothes in a space of her own

Make one palp by another hand leaves another letter fail to
earth what it says out walking on skin debris from two
true stories in matters as if we lavish its fine tip on lungs of art
to put a stop to his tread or peg out between ruts
in thin sheen as that eye that glass jar screwed cold and dark in pots
too out all the same with a stump eyed from the window

After midnight it was a baffle or a very good copy in song style
stapled deep with a mist full of blood for free detritus
flooding slides in capital sequence to watch them drive stout posts
bleak to look at into the dark ground the black lightless fen
all about the aims of the front bound in like a literary theory
snarled in rough cuts to earn a living to repudiate

The hoover fades beneath a lethal march off this page
to another partiality from the air against his masks
to form him now in terror forays or shape him in dumps
in flame run half afraid on a floor of damp glass a lip
at fault speaking idle threads down to the bona fide dress
shirt in hand over fist spooning into his face

So would you care to remain here and be consumed
round the neck as the only route downward like a load
of light verse enduring through barrage and fancy filaments
twittering in the ceanothus of invention parcels
air bent into aesthetic shapes of this mercy or that or broken
right apart eaten away starved crushed old mad blind and
stamped on

Later level force embraces anybody if that's true and I agree
with you out of my hands to where the cities are to play power
splashed out in a witness sense, a complex merit one class say
or ever becoming a kind of work out loud burning

it from one end to the other just because of skin declaring decay
       that might be a view from nowhere but a day in the country

What was made by us is hanging about covered in ribbons and
                                 birdshit
       and aprons all set on this time of night for any other way
                              through
tangles of a seedy mind to hold nothing touched or even true
       to the same life just a door step away from a sheepish mouth
munching a sliver of something carmine and ludicrously
       pastoral as fishpaste or cracks full of dust or an entire bowl

Don't nod or scramble so ruefully for dupes or lying for the poor
       furtive moon-blush army come again try the view alone
odour of almonds am here am you we're a monstrous pair of crows
       doubting summer's purchase a blush in a garden of gleams
sow seeds by the aunt clair path sow the wind in the tender cedar
       rush light charm above the door dilapidated its charm raddled

And see off a dumb tally over a long night's counting till the sun
       glides the new sand sole account crowned legendary and lost
a film a few saw sheepishly on a blank promise to be better after it
       gilded inside to do as we go into the barrier on a face opens
the book of wishes and glides illegible as badgers in a complex pattern
       buried a bad label a gesture or tab shawl they'd like to escape
                                from

Ignore o secure relief fluid at your age one exists or leaves and will
       dissolve by final flux over you unaided inflicted and not once
                              more
be ever one we hear so much and weep at windows in lost sentences
       ignored in the forests. The words on one level condemn us to
                              death
of the use of them as we must simply know the part in the whole
       devoted to a singular being without being which there's
                           nothing left.

Highly Commended Poems

Rachael Allen

Many Bird Roast

I came in, dandy and present
arguing for a moratorium on meat
of the kind splayed out on the table, legs akimbo
like a fallen-over ice skater skidding on her backside
there are dogs in the outhouse and all over the world
that we do not eat
and one small sparrow in a pigeon in a grouse in a swan
that we will certainly eat
overlooking all the drama, with as many eyes as a spider
that we'll cut in two
and the compacted layers of the various meats
will fall away dreamily as a rainbow melts down
into the marsh where it came from
slipping meat from the bone
onto a specially designed knife
there's a call out for plates
I'm the only one with a sense of outcry
someone says, *you weren't like this when it was broiling away*
smelling like your history, smelling like
the deep skin on your knee grazed after playing in the sun all day
skinned with good dirt and your under-blood just showing through
smelling like warm dry firs after burning and the outdoors
after fireworks and Novembers after tea
you eat and smell like the rest of us, dirty rat under your armpit
dirty bird in your stomach
and birds fell down through the chimney with thwacks into buckets
and we got so poor we had to eat them too
strange cockatoos and once a brilliantly lit pure white dove
that we kept in a hutch with a small pot of ink
and when we let it out
it wasn't so much a raven as just a plain black dove
ready to cook, and with superstition, I learnt to.

Simon Armitage

I Kicked a Mushroom

and then I felt bad.
And not just some cute toadstool or gnome's bed
but a fruiting body of brain-coloured disks
as wide as a manhole cover or bin lid,
a raft of silky caps basted in light rain
stemming from one root as thick as a wrist,
anchored in deep earth, like a rope on a beach.
One jab with a spade would have done the job,
then a pitchfork to hoik it over the hedge,
but I stuck in the boot then walked away
with its white meat caught in my tongue and lace.
All night it lies on the lawn inside out,
its tripes and corals turned to the stars,
gills in the air, showing the gods what I am.

Rachael Boast

Coda: Lost Poem

From the other side of the river
softening into that hour
when the scent is released like wine
left to breathe on a mirrored tabletop
it looks as though I have the right idea,
sitting on the boat reading a book,
but it's not so. I keep on with the task
of rewriting the lost poem that turned
mirrors into water and moonlight
into mirrors and water into all manner
and forms of forgetfulness.
The book is merely a cover. Inside it,
the slow work of love, errata of desire,
something written over what is written there.

Andrea Brady

Salthouse

You are softness   suspended
in the edgy air,   oh corporal
of selection   noises.   And you touch
the dust makes patterns   in creases,
whorled and deep   and heavy as a nautilus.
Succeeded by your others   illuminators
creationists paled and flattened   by the need
for sleep, we watch them   mistake
midnight's cockerel and   shoe
the snake in hooves.   They watch us
like white wolves   cattish and   healthy
in trees. In the depth   which is still
our lives, own, we   melt   and frost
making our centre   a certaine
knot of peace.   These limbs   your reach
harden and rooted   in elective ground,
the fathoms vibrate with monsters   overwhelmed
push yourself up from the dive   you are now
running with melted sugar   and close
your primitive organs,   dry yourself
and take back yourself   across that broken bridge.

Alan Buckley

Scum

15/04/89

I lay on the turf, under a steely sky.
No one picked my pockets. No one pissed
on me. The copper who gave me the kiss
of life wasn't beaten up. I died,
that's the truth; and though I'd never known
such closeness, our bodies like beans in a can,
when the air was squeezed from me I died alone.

That's all changed. The words we'd sung as fans
became our bond. We've walked, the ninety-six,
through parish halls, hushed stadiums, and courts.
Now we walk back through time. Something sticks
in our throats. You're at your desk, lost in thought,
scanning a page of lies you'll say is true.
What's the headline that can trumpet this?

Look up. We're standing right in front of you;
what burns in us is fierce as any sun.
That word you want to use. It's on your lips.
Say it to our faces, one by one.

Elizabeth-Jane Burnett

from **Swims**

'*A dictionary would start from the point at which it would no longer give the meanings but the tasks of words.*'

Bataille

To Swim   To give
up.
To disappear.
To appear
in Vanity Fair before breakfast
to afterwards destroy economy of Greece.[1]
To float.
To pierce film lid between air and water.
To explode outwards.
To be an assemblage.
To flower
in the wrong place   to be in the wrong
            place.
To drift.
To not advance capitalism.
To grow in a hedge.
To be lichen.
To be at once
in the body
and under

[1] Christine Lagarde, Managing Director of the International Monetary Fund, explains how she starts the day with swimming in 'Christine Lagarde: Et si c'était elle?' *Vanity Fair France*, December 2014.

and over it.
To sink
and to get back up.
To spread tail feather
in display of bone
to be closer to skeleton and totally fine
what's the worst that could happen

already fallen
already wet
already missing

from the earth but recoverable always
there is something left

to be dug up
to be eaten
to be stolen

there is something left always when words are at
their fullest stretch
something left that cannot be taken.
To not being taken.

John Burnside

The Lazarus Taxa

'Still they stood,
A great wave from it going over them,
As if the earth in one unlooked-for favour
Had made them certain earth returned their love.'
Robert Frost

If anything is safe
to love, it is

the jellyfish, *Aurelia aurita*,
that pink and silver

moon-cloud, drifting wild
in every harbour from the South

Atlantic
to the Bay of Reykjavik;

or *Hippocampus*,
monstrous to the Greeks,

though shaped like horses,
gentle as the wind

in August:
moving softly through

the weeds, the brood male
gathers the eggs in his pouch

like treasure, while the female swims away
to miles of seagrass; coral;

predators.
              If anything is safe
to love, it has to be

the Starry Smooth-Hound,
gliding through the bright

salt water, innocent
of need, its joys

too quick to be remembered
or betrayed.

I would not choose the Bluefin
Tuna, Hector's

Dolphin, or the Humphead
Wrasse.
              Right Whale, Blue Whale, Fin

Whale, Yangtze Finless
Porpoise, and the Maltese Ray

are equally unpromising,
(they will not be here long).
                        In years to come,

the market will experience
a glut in holy relics, scraps of bone

and slivers of dubious tissue, hermetically sealed
in ampoules, with old diagrams

of how things would have looked
had they survived,

convenient gifts
for those who would believe

that absence is its own
reward, a cybernetic

fiefdom of Saxon
gold, the cold

dead-end
as hallows.

If any man were safe
to love, it would be

Lazarus, awake between two worlds,
until a word recalls him from the field

where he had strayed, bereft of song and flight
(no live birds in that place, no

parakeets or hooded orioles;
only the script of Archaeopteryx

consigned, but not reduced
to blueprint

in the marled folds
of hereafter).

The moment he turns,
he finds the world transformed,

the animals he knew, the ox, the ass,
the cattle in the fields, the flocks

of vultures over bloody Golgotha,
all gone, and in their place

a host of resurrections, long-lost
fishes, given up

for dead,
amphibians

and mammals, skipper flies
and pine voles come to life

forever, as he blindly makes his way
through gardens of round-leafed birch

and café marron, the fountains
teeming with Black Kokanee,

painted frogs,
Latimeria

chalumnae, Latimeria
menadoensis

and, out in the furthest shade
of the jellyfish trees,

Mahogany Gliders,
calling his name in the dark,

as if, for now,
the earth returned his love.

Michelle Cahill

The End of the Dream

after Wallace Stevens' 'Of Mere Being'

You squint, turning the pages of a quarterly,
half-dozing, in and out of centre, well beyond
the Socratic itch or the circadian persuasions.
Look over your shoulder, a gesture held by dusk
to observe no gold-fangled bird but a palm tree
raking the fragile skies, singular and eternal –
with a movement so discreet it begins to thread
the light, you are almost stunned not by melancholy
but the hallucinatory moment years have spent.

Frogs moan, eucalypts pixelate in dark stirrings
that come much later; and should a formal music
drop it would be a flat line in reason's anaesthetic bed.
You remember the stained glass, cathedral pines,
fragrant star jasmine infuse the pages of a culture war,
there are hunger games and Israel blitzing Palestine.
Unfamiliar rooms inhabited, a Fushan sandalwood
rinses the air, the scalene triangle of three solicitors,
all sides unequal, a tenant needing a dog-proof fence.
Now your ex-boy is a landlord, your mother's body
dry and papery like snakeskin shed past midnight
when a bird with tawny feather hair extensions quips.
At the end of the dream, a garden bench presumes
the child has outgrown you, a jacaranda shakes her thick,
purple amnesia, predicting what makes us happy
                                        or unhappy.

Vahni Capildeo

Blood

Look, sir, I bleed.
You're asking, where's the villain? Look, I bleed.
When men bleed, they shouldn't.
Men bleed when they shouldn't.
There are too many women in this play,
all of an age to bleed; none bore children.
Lunar and silent, they have spread a field
of blood beneath the action. Dirt has skirts,
smooth roads rust, tiled surfaces tainted
with vinegar; nothing wipes nothing out,
nothing can be reached directly; nothing
that does not shed a lining, shudder, rubbish
the chance to make one clean sweet queen bee line.
Look, sir. The whole tree of myself blushes
for your attention, came into flowering,
and was cut down; flowered again, cut down
again, not by a blade or breeze; the natural
result of inattention. Yours. The sea
breaks its allotted surface and self-harms,
changing where it goes, what can live inside it.
You'll buy me a new shirt. Hire people
to wipe up after me. I want their job:
want my blood on my hands, and in your eyes.

Becky Cherriman

Jesus Lives

Jesus has treacly eyes and lives in my granny's spare room.
When we come to visit, this is where we sleep.
There's panelling on the walls, a tottering wardrobe
and a mahogany bed, corrugated at the foot. It's huge.
Put it this way, the BFG has nothing on this bed.

My sister says Jesus's eyes are evil.
I say he's sad because we don't believe in him
but jump just as high at the stair's sudden crack.

It's Granny, juggling lumpy hot water bottles;
she leans on feather pillows, offers talcum-kissed cheeks.
Then, the chime of a ghost bell!
Granny's dead school mistress ringing for her
as she returns downstairs for ginger beer.

We go back to considering Jesus
who thinks he's being helpful by watching over us
at night. Our limbs petrify.

Still, when sleep steals her, I seek out
the answers in those treacly eyes.

Kayo Chingonyi

Alternate Take

When they laid our father out, mwaice wandi,
I want to say – I'm meant to say – soft light
played the skin of his spent face and the sobs
were, of course, a jangling kind of song.

If I could take you where the sandy earth
meets his final stone, tiled and off-white,
we might have learned to worship better gods.
He was known, in the shebeens, as *long John*.

At the wake relatives tried variations
on the words of the day: *I am sorry*
for your grieving/your trouble/your loss.
I've been weighing these apologies for years

that pass and retreat like disused stations.
I think of his walk becoming your quarry,
his knack for beguiling women, your cross.
It's enough to bring me here, past tears

to where his face simplifies to a picture:
the shrine in Nagoya, him stood, sequoia
among lesser trees, looking good in denim;
every inch the charismatic spectre.

In his memory my voice bears his tincture –
saxophone played low / boy raised on soya
porridge, chloroquine, a promise of heaven.
There are days I think I'm only a vector

carrying him slowly to my own graveyard,
and standing at the lectern, rather than my son,
will be another copy: the same sharp
edge to the chin, that *basso profundo* hum.

Kid brother, we breathers have made an art
of negation, see how a buckled drum
is made from a man's beating heart
and a fixed gaze is a loaded weapon.

Theodoros Chiotis

Interference (or, Uncommon Time for the Medicalised Subject)

> *'Those diseases which medicines do not cure, iron cures;*
> *those which iron cannot cure, fire cures;*
> *and those which fire cannot cure,*
> *are to be reckoned wholly incurable.'*
> Hippocrates, *Aphorisms* section VII, 87

The removal & rearrangement
  of letters to make
    new words & names
for the altered (but not new) body:
an endeavour
that was never   going to be
  entirely successful.

The flame singes the hairs
just above the lip   as the order is repeated.
You dress the wound
with language: this way,
the body is convinced
of its new necessities -
        those childhood rhymes
  you learnt as an adult:

"Ring-a-ring-a-roses,
A pocket full of posies;
Ashes! Ashes!
We all fall down!"

You now have to train yourself
to look at me
as if I am no longer there.

The watchword resurfaces
when the clatter
of the machines
alters time &
substitutes the body:
"All irregularities
    will be handled
by the
    forces governing each
                    dimension".

The needle punctures my skin:
    the shot is punctuated
by the snapping
of the middle finger and the thumb
 at that exact moment -
a hairline fracture
across the side
of my left arm.

When we have sex after
the needle has been safely disposed of,
I can only see letters
falling on the floor -
a series of corridors
leading to wrong rooms:
    "What we have left we put in the pot".

Like a robotic mannequin
    [alas, I will never become an android]
I learn to unpin and pin my eyes onto
a series of interchangeable skulls.

Acronyms erode multiplicities:
    this is not me rifling
through this new language I am
swallowing

                    and/or
injecting;
this is the memory of
my grandmother's multiple
strokes, her face incandescent
with words as big as planets,
her face a vision of
a sky opening out into geometries
of flesh and fibres,
geometries that
fold
      &
let off
fireworks
charring black
the soft hillocks underneath
the skin.

Even if you don't turn around
 as you climb
the long staircase,
               the axons will still combust
      & wither.

You are then taught to let
language interfere with yr
                              body.
You are taught to
tick the empty boxes.
You are taught to admit that
these feet are made to
drag across cobbled pavement.
You are taught to rearrange the letters:
    your outer velocity decreases
as accretion disks
    become points of reference
on the star maps across the dark of the body.

When the book starts
to burn yr
            legs,
fear becomes a

                                    question and

ontology becomes a
      field trip into
refractory junctions.

Shame -
unlike
            Perec,
      you
can no longer
      drop an
      E.

Maya Chowdhry

Butterfly Orchid

I don't remember how I came to be snaring the mossy scales of the Golden Oak in the Gorson forest, or why I know those names.

I remember a dream where I was dust floating in water-saturated air.

I don't remember waking up in bright sunshine.

I remember stretching and breathing, seeing delicate black flowerheads tumbling below me. I remember a sweet shiny smell and feeling I had all the time in the world to grow.

I don't remember my flowerheads shrinking, shrivelling and falling to the forest floor.

I remember summer rain drenching my black petal faces so insects came to watch the circus.

I don't remember how summer ended.

I remember my flower tips drying out to wizened hollow stumps and me shrinking inside, storing energy in my roots, retracting to stillness. I remember the echo of a rain quail call the dawn back from darkness.

I don't remember when I became deaf.

I remember the silent beats of water drops on the canopy and all I could hear was chlorophyll.

I don't remember this blindness of shimmering hollow blackness.

I remember watching a Pritha spider scurrying across its shadow, wearing night into day.

I don't remember not feeling my root tips drinking in water, breathing the scent of a tree.

Elisabeth Sennitt Clough

Boy

Because I wasn't his son, I stepped up to *Boy*,
        anchored myself to the name's brute strength:
        all the hack and heft of it, the call to graft
over fence posts, firewood, sacks of coal.

During those minutes, we didn't speak
        beyond the saw or grip or wrench of a task.
        We were reduced to two pairs of working hands,
our palms ungloved, nails rimmed with grime.

From her station at the kitchen window
        peeling veg, my mother kept up the charade
        with a nod, a smile when our eyes met,
her grey hair masked by a scarf.

One morning, I tried to urinate standing up,
        my fingers squeezing two folds of skin
        as I tried to channel the water. I straddled
the bowl: hands, legs, floor glistening.

Later, I held a mirror between my thighs,
        pulled back the velvet flesh and found a shoot
        of pink pushing through the frills –
at last a nub of boy.

Kelvin Corcoran

At the Hospital Doors

The sun shines on the Oncology Centre,
the red cars, the grey, the marked-out spaces;
workmen to the site office, patients to reception,
paces vary with purpose at the sliding doors.

Wind from the distant world sifts the borders
and the light lifts but there's no revelation here,
the working night turns into the working day,
deliveries arrive, innocent cells race deranged.

Pain seeps down into faults below ground,
grips the roots of trees with blackened fingers,
sounds every note of diving bird song
and directs the shifting clouds not to speak.

Guided by certain hands and quiet talk,
around whose neck are these pearls arrayed?
Little aria little aria in the streets of dark town,
out in the hollows the air of Autumn sings.

*

Three ghosts sing for life
from the white sheets of final care.

I was born in 1920 – I married when?
and then the war, three sons I had, my boys,
my brother died when I was ten,
it grieves me still, that something unfinished.

Well that was me working on the farm,
me and my dad, up the hills, the best school;
though she left me, I love her even still
but oh my daughter's the pillar of my life.

The year? I don't remember. I'll ask Alan,
ah – no, I can't can I, he's gone now
but we had fun, hungry most of the war,
the Mediterranean, salt water out of the taps.

Two women and a man sing for life
moment by moment from their beating hearts,
the miracle of ordinary events recalled
– oh but I miss him, all gone I know.

*

We lie in common secluded, curtained for surgery,
paused on the threshold for time to be removed.

I hear a man close-by weighing his life thus far,
hear his words hit the cold pan of the scales.

Let the sincerity in his heart, lighter than a feather
open the doors from the light and from the dark.

Keki Daruwalla

In night country

1

she is so ephemeral
she is ephemera herself
alights
      for a precipitous moment
      on nerve-edge
         dream-edge,
dream that darkens into a forest
where only shadows thrive

steps
      for one luminous moment
      on that rim
          where consciousness and amnesia
      meet and vanish
      blur and meet

she has almost become invisible
the plough can't reach her under the furrow
though dealers in the occult
  have seen her image
         splash for a moment in deep wells

2

when you are neglected for three millennia
      you retire underground
             one with the seedling's
     long night of germination

     long-bearded messiahs
drove you under the earth—
      the ones who thought they had a direct line

to Him, the maker of planets,
                        marker of orbits,
a hot line to the manufacturer of stars.
                        they hadn't heard
of black holes, comets and quasars
or these too would be in our scriptures.

3
groves were sacred to her, they say
now axe and saw mill work overtime there

old bards, high
on hash and cannabis
could lasso her with an incantation;
        but old bards are gone
                        and so is their music

some lucky ones have heard your silks rustle
(the hem always beyond reach)
                    they haven't seen you, unsure
                    if that wasn't the wind in the cedars

a sibyl once said it's not
that She won't reveal herself
it's that they are
        afraid of her revelation

4
yet as the year waxes and the dying winter
moves past the thaw ooze
we find her voice in the songbird's throat;
at dusk in lapwing country,
the cacophonic lapwing country,
                    one senses her presence.

and somewhere in a dark crypt of our psyche
unknown to ourselves

there is a small hooded flame
that belongs to her, she, grain-giver
barley-goddess, goddess of word and melody

Rishi Dastidar

What's the matter with
[insert (non-metropolitan) English constituency of choice]?

with apologies to Thomas Frank

It's as if we still have whiplash
from that brainbreaking exit poll,
accurately pointing to the crash:
voteless dreams exacting a toll.
What now for a nation fissiparous?
No chance this lot'll be magnanimous.
The things we've in common they forget,
loosening the straps of the safety net.
But there is light when we look round,
(their brand is not detoxified,
hence why their supporters are shy)
if we leave the moral high ground.
Forget complain-

*Look I'll go back and finish the sonnet in a bit, but
seriously can you please stop calling people who voted to
the right of you* evil? *They're not – ill-informed maybe,
only looking as far as their front door or their street, but
they are not baby eaters. If you start in that register, how
can you ever hope they might listen to you when you try
and win them back? I have been on the left long enough to
know that a cry of betrayal is never far away, but it's really
not a good look to suggest that it was the voters wot did
the stabbing in the front. And don't take this to mean that
I am any less committed to social justice – I voted Labour,
I gave money to the campaign, hell I cried on election
night – but seriously, we can sit around bemoaning all the
forces arrayed against us, or we can work with the grain
of England to try and find this fabled progressive majority*

that still might be out there. I'll take ends over means most
days if we can save what we have before starting again.
Practically? Hell I don't know, but we have to get out
from behind our screens and in to the world. As it turns
out that's still where politics lives – who knew? And when
we're out there, let us try treating it as a carnival of joy
instead of a festival of I-Told-You-So-ism, served with a
side of slathering vitriol. Rationality isn't enough, harping
on about how our values are superior isn't enough – put
some fizz in your pieties! Fuck it, rebrand the Welfare State
as the Welfare Trampoline if you like, but Jesus we will
not win if we do not offer something that looks like a smile
wrapped around the weapons we'll need to fight the fear we
know is coming. Right, done. Kthnxbai.

-ing, we need to persuade;
the new Jerusalem has only been delayed.

May 2015

US Dhuga

Philoctetes at the Gym

No compunction, my physiotherapist
Walks, kale juice in hand, out of The Raw Chemist

With the swagger of a Neoptolemus
Who will lie to me, to you, to all of us

For the sake of winning what he mythifies
As our battle. I watch him pause, flex his thighs,

Take a single, discreet white Pall Mall
(Charcoal filtered) from his Nike carryall.

I tighten the brace back round my ankle
Wondering if and when we're setting sail.

Today the pain in my foot is bearable,
Not so my personnel.

Douglas Dunn

Class Photograph

Renfrew High School, 1956

We were Elizabethan girls and boys,
Too young for politics, too old for toys.
Then Hungary and Suez changed all that,
Or so it feels in tired old retrospect.
Nostalgia corrodes the intellect.
It makes you want to eat your coat and hat.

One foot in childhood, one in adolescence,
Rock Around the Clock made far more sense
Even than *The Battle of the River Plate* –
Stiff upper lips and Royal Navy dash,
Its Technicoloured brio and panache
Heroic, gore-less, brilliant, out of date.

Like Ovaltineys in their Start-rite shoes –
It catches up on you, it really does,
This looking back, this old class photograph.
Be-blazered in our uniforms and ties
(*Who he? Who she?*) – pensioners in disguise
As who they were, a pictured epitaph.

Pillar-boxes still red (though not much else is)
And the scarcely visible orthodoxies
All still in place, plus global urgency,
Destructive wars abroad … And yet, God bless
Democracy, dissent, and the NHS
Which underpins our civic decency.

Steve Ely

Jerusalem

Pathfinder – Doncaster, Dearne. Old Street
in Elmet, from Strafford to Tanshelf via Beacon.
And did those feet? Agricola, Hengist,
the ceorl in charge of the king's gerfalcon.
Muck between the toes, Holy Communion.
Cross on Lound Lane at the fork to Rat Hall,
forward to Hampole and Watlynge Street.
Stump-scratting in bluebells with metal detectors,
endymion non-scripta. Rusted shire-shoe,
crown of the witch-pricking king. Skrying in wheel ruts
and livers of badgers. Deerhounds hammering
lazerlit pastures. Yommer with spade
and crowbar. Brock-rotted stromatolite reef.

John Foggin

A Weak Force

There's sometimes a loss you can't imagine;
the lives never lived by your children, or
by the one who simply stopped
in the time it takes
to fall to the ground
from the top of a tower block.

They say gravity is a weak force.
I say the moon will tug a trillion tons
of salt sea from its shore.
I say a mountain range will pull a snowmelt
puddle out of shape.
I say gravity can draw a boy
through a window
and into the air.

There is loss no one can imagine.

In the no time between
falling and not falling
you learned the art of not falling;

beneath you burned
the lights of Sheepscar, Harehills,
Briggate, Vicar Lane;
lights shone in the glass arcades,
on the tiles, on the gantries of tall cranes;
motorway tail lights trailed ribbons of red,
and you were far beyond falling.

Because you shut your eyes
because you always shut your eyes
you closed them tight as cockleshells
because when you did that the world

would go away the world
would not see you.

I remember how you ran like a dream.
I remember how you laughed when I swore
I would catch you.

Then you flared you went out
you flared like a moth and you blew
away over the lights over the canal
the river the sour moors the cottongrass
the mills of the plain
and over the sea and over the sea
and the bright west
and you sank like the sun.

Miriam Gamble

The Oak That Was Not There

The oak that was not there was not there
and the sands went walking under the sea.

The clocks went forward, the clocks went back.
Someone lost their temper with me.

From a hillock, we looked on as water
swept its grey silk garment through the estuary.

The clocks went forward, the clocks went back.
The penitent, down on his knees, begged

for the honey of forgiveness from a round god
whose presence we had proven.

The clocks went forward, the clocks went back;
there was no response. But we must act responsibly!

said our grave leader as the flowers of the machair
grew scissor faces. On their faces,

the hands of the second went chop, chop, chop;
the digitalis ate a mink. To think,

one murmured, That it should come down to this.
Another nodded: I consent there is something wrong –

as the blown-glass nimbi angled and clinked
and the clocks went back and forwards, back and forwards –

Where is the oak, for one thing? Where is the blasted oak?
And the round god fell from the sky like a fish.

Philip Gross

Back

Just a wish out of place – the first click
      starts a ticking backwards: one pop of a pod
          of balsam, like a caught breath, like a sigh

in-sucked, and its blush-blooms, in popsicle-pink
      and all over us briefly, start acting their age
          now, retracting their flip asides; they shrink

into something like shame. Go dark
      like a playhouse in Puritan times. The buddleia
          shrugs off its easy disconnected butterflies.

But this will be nothing to the tearing
      up, the snap-crackling of roots. First that sad
          defeated carnival of rhododendrons (and who

would defend *them*?) herded from the hills; then
      the other non-natives, one by one… The pears
          may try to merge in with the apples, yes,

the crabbiest of them, until they're denounced
      and we'll wake to the rumble of the sycamores
          retreating; London planes stripped of the name,

leaving squares bare and pitted. They make for the sea,
      hoping to unpick the trade routes, wind the tides
          back, all the accidents that brought them…

Now the lights are going out all over
      Europe's gardens. Bird migrations locked out.
          Silence deep enough to catch the drift

like smoke, like snow, of the murmur of gone
           approaching: wildfowl flowing south, the grunt
                and lowing of the ice sheet crumpling into place.

Almost as if we'd wished it. As if it had never been away.

Jodie Hollander

Dream of a Burning Woman

Every night I'd say good-bye to my mother
walking in her long nightgown into the fire;

her hair waving behind her as she entered
a cave with a black mouth and orange embers

burning on the ground. This was that place
she must have believed was her real home.

I never asked her why she had to go there,
knew only that this was where she always slept.

Each morning, I'd tiptoe over to her,
never quite sure if I'd find her dead or alive—

But she was always there, wrapped in a blanket,
so I'd pull her close, and say she hadn't died,

say I was proud this woman was my mother,
and had made it through another night alive.

Wayne Holloway-Smith

Some Waynes

Magic Wayne with flowers; Wanye West; Box-of-Tricks Wayne;
Wayne sad on Facebook, proving he loves his daughter; the
sporty Wayne – loves himself skinny; Bald Wayne, head like a
rocking chair; Amy Waynehouse; Wayne the ironic; Fat Wayne
– tits pushed beneath a Fred Perry Wayne; Wayne from near
Slough; Ugly Wayne – the unlikely mess of his wife Wayne –
canned laughter; Wayne who renamed another Wayne fleabag;
Track-suited Wayne – your hubcaps, his pockets; Home and
A-Wayne; Randy Wayne; Wayne, fountains of him, every drop
snug to someone's mum; Wayne, boyfriend of Stacey; Wayne
-ker; Wayne the rap star, gold teeth, grime; Wayne the Superhero;
Wayne the Cowboy; Dancing Wayne – in tights; It's-Wayning-
Men; a cavalcade of Waynes fucking each other up in a Geoff
Hattersley poem – in a pub, in Barnsley; Purple Wayne;
Wayne's World Wayne; Wayne 'Sleng Teng' Smith; A-Wayne
in a Manger; all of them have stopped what they're doing, all
of them divided in two rows and facing each other, all of them,
arms raised, they are linking fingers, all of them: an architrave
through which I celebrate, marching like I am the bridegroom,
grinning like I am the bride

Rosalind Jana

Hollow

He was a dent in the sofa,
hollowed to fit in the corner;
at the other end, two dips: heels left in felt.

We could not fill these cavities.
Only his stoop might –
elbows sagging into cushions each morning.
We sat in other places,
avoided the shadows cast
by our father.
He left himself behind, dwindled
to blank eyes, trembling hands.

Fearing the January cold
he bound the living room round with heat
thick as boiled wool, tight at the neck.

"I'm sorry," he said, "so sorry."
Our chatter tried to fill his gaps.
We edged through days, orbited the empty space
of absence.

Our mother stacked his walking boots
under stairs.
His overcoat hung in the dark,
velvet collar waiting for a warm body
to fill it up.

He tried to fold himself away,
but could not curl small enough
to pass unseen.

Dust settled as days passed; months marked by
deeper hollows until, with such slowness
of bare twigs edging into leaf,
cool air spooled the house.

Upholstery dents receded.
We pulled on coats, slipped feet in boots,
and took small steps
imprinting softly into hills.

Zaffar Kunial

Prayer

First heard words, delivered to this right ear
Allah hu Akbar – God is great – by my father
in the Queen Elizabeth maternity ward.
God's breath in man returning to his birth,
says Herbert, is prayer. If I continued

his lines from there, from *birth* – a break Herbert
chimes with *heav'n and earth* – I'd keep in thought
my mum on a Hereford hospital bed
and say what prayer couldn't end. I'd say
I made an animal noise, hurled language's hurt

at midday, when word had come. Cancer. Now so spread
by midnight her rings were off.
                            I stayed on. At her bed.
Earlier, time and rhythm flatlining, I whispered
Thank you   I love you   thank you
                            mouth at her ear.
She stared on, ahead. I won't know if she heard.

Shara McCallum

Vesta to Madwoman

Was a time I thought to extinguish flames,
but blue tongues licked at the edges of sleep,

waking me to strike that first match.
So, yes, I was an arsonist.

But have you considered destruction
is kin to desire?

The ruined and those that ruin
require each other, the way fire

needs oxygen to light. A blaze
razes a field without thought and, I admit,

sometimes you were that field.
But, my girl, look what this has sown in you:

to know what is sifted from ash
is lit by the embers of disaster.

Niall McDevitt

Lithostrotos

aim for the Lithostrotos, the rock where Pilate quizzed Jesus, other levels 2000 years too high, aim for the arc of Ecce Homo, veer up the Nun's Ascent even as Arab boys charge down like laughing armies, enter the doorway on your left and pay a few shekels, it will go to the good sisters of Notre Dame de Sion, pass through the central hall where a group of charismatics is ululating—hallelujahs and glossolalias—then enter the caverns... suddenly you are elsewhere in time-space, there are rocks and ropes, opaque cells, the echoing drip of a 2000-year-old cistern once part of the Struthion Pool, a Roman 'bullet' the size of a football, and great slabs of multi-coloured stone, some striated with jagged lines to stop horses from slipping, red stones, gold stones, green stones, grey stones, curvy and glossy, magnificent reliefs, but the mural of Jesus on matching painted striations with crown of thorns, red robe and cross, is a too hygienic daub

'this' says a falcon-eyed guide to two lachrymose women 'is the only place Jesus walked'

(but it's not! it was built by Hadrian a century after Christ) anyway ... here come the charismatics, they won't be worried about datelines either

the Lithostrotos, the Gabbatha, the Stone Pavement, I had always sought the idea of the Stone Pavement, a symbol of urbanity, hoping to walk somewhere or nowhere or anywhere and find a literary magic as antidote to the black magic of history, but this depends on the truth, a Stone Pavement founded on truth

Momtaza Mehri

Portrait Of An Intimate Terrorist In His Natural Habitat

In the animal kingdom, bright pigment can signify poison,
toxicity or anything else read as amber, as warning.
You walk into the room in red Air Jordans,
lean as a prophecy, and pretend it's an accident.
I heard Armageddon will require smart casual.
We've been preparing.

I peel away from conversations about myself
like the skin of a grape. Never ask for much.
Just a sleep loose as pennies, a house for hooyo,
a soil that won't spit her back. A man will love you
like a horse running out of a burning building.
The old women said it best, sang it best.

A lipstick smudge on your knuckles, the same colour as roadkill.
Alarm bells can be set on vibrate. For you, more than once.
We can do this both ways.
Meaning, we started a space race of our own.
Whoever nicks the other first,
names the colour of the stain.

Jessica Mookherjee

Ursa Minor

Four thousand and seventy four friends on Facebook.
Pout-perfect teenager, touching me through
a laptop.

Just before her bud-burst, she sent me
a Friend Request, status update,
she dreamt a bear ate her last night.

Poor Callisto, running to forest-mother,
don't talk to strangers until you get there.
Who do you think the bear was? I ask her.

In her dream, she lived in a house of glass,
inside the woods, seen by bears, seen by wolves.

Outside, he watches her, clicks on her posts,
likes her pictures of new hairstyles,
picnics and drinks with friends.
A gust of hot breath on glass,
broken screen. Teeth marks.

The shock of being so new, so ripe.
I typed: love sometimes eats us up.
We are all animals in moonlight.

Callisto, LOL, smiley face, heart,
don't go into the woods to be torn apart.
She replies: I think the bear was my friend.

Later I look as she posts a picture of her bedroom.
Pink like a cot-cloth, guarded by her teddy-bear,
I see a thousand likes.

Paul Muldoon

Walnuts

1

Bringing to mind the hemispheres of the brain in the brainpan,
these walnut halves are as ripe
for pickling now as in 860, the dye in a Viking girl's under-dress
then being derived from walnut husks. I hear you stifle
a yawn when I note that steamed
black walnut is generally held to be inferior to kiln-dried
while the term *à la mode de Caen*
refers specifically to the braising of tripe
in apple cider. I who have been at the mercy of the cider-press
have also been known to trifle
with the affections of a dryad in a sacred grove,
a judge's daughter and a between-maid to Lord Mountbatten
among others from beyond my clan.
It was only as recently as 1824 we first used the term 'to snipe'.
Walnut was the go-to stock wood for both Brown Bess
and the Lee-Enfield bolt-action, magazine-fed, repeating rifle.
Each has seen service on the shores of Lough Erne
in the hands of both wood-kernes and followers of the First Earl.

2

Our own interpersonal relationships have tended to be so askew
it was only as recently as 1844 we first used the term 'scarf'
of the neck-garter. Girding up the loins
for a family feud has often proved a more fecund
line of inquiry. Walnuts are now deemed
good against malignancies of breast and prostate – not only tried
but tried and true. From time to time you
and I have met on a windswept airfield or wharf
where we've seen fit to join
battle without ever having reckoned

on how the Irish law on treasure trove
would change in the light of the Derrynaflan paten
never mind King Sitric being the son-in-law of King Brian Boru
who prevailed over him at Clontarf
or, at the Boyne,
William of Orange's putting paid to his father-in-law, James II.
It was at the Boyne, you recall, that Ahern
gave Paisley the 'peace bowl' turned from a local walnut-burl.

André Naffis-Sahely

Postcard from the Cape

for Declan Ryan and Rachael Allen

Few feet
tread the tired timber floors
of the old Observatory now, a couple
of tourists perhaps, or the odd
data analyst skulking in slippers
down the dark musty corridors.
The security guard is reading *The Pleasure Tube*,
'an exhilarating conspiracy aboard a sexy starship'.

There's no
star-gazing tonight and the clouds
stalk the yellow moon like hungry hyenas.
In 1820, when the Cape had that wet
smell of fever about it, Fearon Fallows
decided his work should devour his life,
and six years after his wife and children had died
he installed his telescope atop Slangkop,

or Snake Hill,
as the Dutch colonists called it.
It's getting late, and the runaways
from the Valkenberg have grown hungry.
Little to eat today, just like yesterday too...
A few streets away, the Malay muezzin
clears his throat for the prayer call at the mosque
down in Salt River, past invisible lines

no whites
dare to cross. It's safer indoors,
inside panic mansions with Alsatians

and ARMED RESPONSE signs. David Shook
is in town – one night only! – on his way
to the lush land of Burundi, where the districts
are carved into mountains and the mayors
are 'king of the hill'. He tips an espresso

into a tall Coke –
'Haitian coffee,' he says – and we discuss
how travel can harden the heart, inure it
to pity and pain…When dawn breaks,
I go into the garden and watch Devil's Peak
glow like a live coal. My myopia grows worse,
all I see is a blaze – but who needs high definition?
If I close my eyes, the whole world feels like home.

Daljit Nagra

Father of Only Daughters

Thousand times or more tonight
now you're in a big-girl bed
and it's mum's rare night out
I've simply flown upstairs

to watch you upside down again.
I'm so *oh* over my head
knowing you're safe at this stage
behind your bed-guard.

Two years old, already a clown,
you're the jumping sidekick
to your bigger sister
who's kicked off her duvet again.

In my past, I was treated
as a child when I was a man
and forced to remain in wedlock
to uphold the family name.

Look at me flying upstairs
on the wings of my shame
for my second-chance life.
A life under yours in a fall.

Miriam Nash

The Father's Caesarean

When it's all over with the stepmother, the father rents a flat
in a converted hospital. So much to hear now, he sleeps alert,
tuned to the scud of passing trucks and crackle of the pipes.

Some nights, he's visited by the ghosts of surgeons
who still go about their shifts on the old wards:
women, prodding his stomach with their stethoscopes.

Aren't you the lucky one, they say, *we are the very best,*
schooled in the modern ways. He can sense their breath,
the coolness of a glove, a drift of knife. Tonight

he comes to, mid-procedure: hands inside him; edges,
separations, weight. Something umbilical moves in his skin
and all his body is a voice that calls and calls until they lift

each of his children out of him: not babies, but small,
bundled in hats and scarves. The street is full of foxes' yells.
The surgeons lay the children on their father's chest.

Charlotte Newman

All that Jazz

Duff credit card exact size of visor.
Nothing to see/hear save for the slattern
scurry of slutty children, neatly boxed
centre square; parental advisory
cusped by husbanded blinkers. The kids cling
to dad, judge in the High Court of Lahore,
whose credit doth abhor the things his kids
once wore. Much more like you, who, then unstoned,
fleshed Al-Jazeera hip-wise from our side;
your side mere forbidden fruit for the weird
men leering from the window the wrong side
of the car stuck stubborn in a non-pro-
verbial rut. Maximise the freedom
of uncovered eyes: turn flesh into hard pulp fact.

Sean O'Brien

One Way or Another

One way or another at this late stage
I must have them all back, those lost afternoons
In the hawthorn wood on the quarry floor
With the scent like piss, like Shalimar,
With the attic also, where love took place,
With the fall of your hair
When you'd marked your page,
Over the pillow and over the grass,
With the look on your face when you called my name
As if that word were entirely new
And I answered in kind
And that was enough, it was world without end.

Where did we go when the old year died?
We eluded ourselves. Where did we hide?
Landfill, riverbed, passage of time,
Somewhere whose name can never be said.
Yet I must trace the stairs again
From the attic room to the quarry floor
Though no such places exist, any more
Than the rain that fell on your sleeping face
When I covered you up
With my coat and saw
The rose-flush fading on your skin,
But not that this was a moment of grace.

What business of ours who are gone
Can it be if the past keeps faith.
If the may-tree's scent and the rain evoke
The lost look on your face when you awoke
In the evening wood, in the attic room,
As if they amount to the true address
Where secretly we're living?

I think on the whole I have nothing to say,
I am old and ill, have gone away.
What is this if not more of the same,
When the merciless ghosts insist
That if I dare listen, I'll hear my name?

Pascale Petit

Mama Amazonica

1

Picture my mother as a baby, afloat
on a waterlily leaf,

a nametag round her wrist –
Victoria amazonica.

There are rapids ahead
the doctors call 'mania'.

For now, all is quiet –
she's on a deep sleep cure,

a sloth clings to the cecropia tree,
a jaguar sniffs the bank.

My mother on her green raft,
its web of ribs, its underside of spines.

I'll sing her a lullaby,
tell her how her quilted crib

has been known to support
a carefully balanced adult.

My newborn mama
washed clean by the drugs,

a caiman basking beside her.

2

All around her the other patients snore
while her eyes open their mandorlas.

Now my mother is turning
into the flower,

she's heating up. By nightfall
her bud opens its petals

to release
the heady scent of pineapple.

How the jungle storeys stir
in the breeze from the window behind her.

She hears the first roar
of the howler monkey,

then the harpy eagle's swoop,
the crash through galleries of leaves,

the sudden snatch
then the silence in the troop.

    3
Haloperidol,
phenobarbital –

they've tried them all
those witch doctors, and still

she leaps up in her green nightie
and fumbles to make tea,

slopping the cup over her bed
like the queen of rain.

See her change from nightclub singer
to giant bloom

in the glow of the nightlight –

a mezzo-soprano
under the red moon.

She's drawing the night-flying scarabs
into the crucible of her mind.

Over and over they land
and burrow into her lace.

By dawn she closes her petals.

    4
All the next day the beetles stay inside her,
the males mount the females,

their claws hooked round forewings.

There is pollen to feed on –
no need to leave their *pension*.

Night after night, my mother
replays this – how the white

lily of her youth
let that scarab of a man

scuttle into her floral chamber
before she could cry no.

She flushes a deep carmine,
too dirty to get up.

And her face releases them –
the petals of her cheeks spring open.

Black beetles crawl out, up the ward walls.

Jacob Polley

Every Creeping Thing

By leech, by water mite
by the snail on its slick of light
    by the mercury wires
    of the spiders' lyres
and the great sound-hole of the night

By the wet socket of a levered stone
by a dog-licked ice cream cone
    by spores, mildew
    by the green *atchoo*
by the yellow split pea and the bacon bone

All the doors must have their way
and every break of day its day
    instead of a soul
    Jackself has a coal
and the High Fireman to pay

By head-lice powder, Paraquat
snapdragon's snap and rat-tat-tat
    who's at the door
    of the door of the door
it's Jackself in his toadskin hat

Nisha Ramayya

Secretions or Obstructions

1

> You come too late, much too late. There will always be
> a world – a white world – between you and us.... The
> other's total inability to liquidate the past once and for all.
> In the face of this affective ankylosis of the white man, it
> is understandable that I could have made up my mind to
> utter my Negro cry. Little by little, putting out pseudopodia
> here and there, I secreted a race. (Fanon 2008: 92)

2

In the face of this affective 'formation of a stiff joint by
consolidation of the articulating surfaces' –

In the face of this affective 'coalescence of two bones originally
distinct' –

It is understandable that I, like a critical rub, could have the
advantage of taking into your skin and the disadvantage of
going off.

You come too late, embarrassed by the analogy between you
and us. You say what doesn't come to mind: 'toasted bread or
potatoes, peat, lignite, withered leaves'.

You say the utterly in common.

There will always be a world in which this self, projecting
inwards or outwards, separates.

Likeness to likeness, we are marrow-scooped in the face of the
articulating surfaces. Chins pointing down to the drops of oil in
backlit water, we give ourselves away.

3

In *On Being Included: Racism and Diversity in Institutional Life*,
Sara Ahmed considers the arrival of the stranger in the university
(she discusses the implicit racialisation of the stranger elsewhere).
In the institutional space, the body of colour is, statistically and
otherwise, the body out of place. Reflecting on her experiences
of working in British and Australian universities, Ahmed writes:
'When an arrival is noticeable, we notice what is around. I look
around and re-encounter the sea of whiteness. I had become so
used to this whiteness that I had stopped noticing it' (2012: 35).

This impression of whiteness is an impression of coherence that
results from a gathering of white bodies; the body of colour
disrupts this coherence:

> It is important to remember that whiteness is not reducible
> to white skin or even to something we can have or be, even
> if we pass through whiteness. When we talk about a 'sea of
> whiteness' or 'white space,' we talk about the repetition
> of the passing by of some bodies and not others. And yet
> non-white bodies do inhabit white spaces; we know this.
> Such bodies are made invisible when spaces appear white,
> at the same time as they become hypervisible when they do
> not pass, which means they 'stand out' and 'stand apart.'
> You learn to fade in the background, but sometimes you
> can't or you don't. (42)

The stranger who wishes to pass – whom Ahmed describes
as 'the "right kind" of minority, the one who aims not to cause
unhappiness or trouble' (157) – tries not to stand out. She
minimises her difference in an attempt to blend into the
surroundings, to reproduce the coherence of the white space
by blending, by fading, by dissolution.

Standing out is the cause and effect of uncomfortable feelings.
The stranger does not like to sit down, for fear that she will be

asked to leave. She does not like to make herself comfortable, for fear that she has misheard the invitation:

> Whiteness is produced as host, as that which is already in place or at home. To be welcomed is to be positioned as the one who is not at home. Conditional hospitality is when you are welcomed on condition that you give something back in return. (43)

What may be given back in return? What may be given in order to return? The intensity of the stranger's gratitude corresponds to the impact of her returns.

4

Frantz Fanon suggests that whiteness is rigidity, brittle coalescence; blackness is projection, extraction, supersaturated release. Ahmed's rendering of the body of colour is similarly obtrusive – a cluster of sore points, swellings and stains.

Although the 'sea of whiteness' implies fluidity, the body of colour may experience the continuous body of whiteness as an obstruction ('like banging your head against a brick wall'):

> Things might appear fluid if you are going the way things are flowing. When you are not going that way, you experience a flow *as* solidity, as what you come up against. In turn, those who are not going the way things are flowing are experienced *as* obstructing the flow. (Ahmed 2012: 186-187)

To come: the incoherence of our bodies is what we bring up, the condition of what we have to bring.

To come up: despite the insufficiencies of the conditions, we don't know when to leave.

To come up against: (the impression of) settling deeply.

5

Kidney stones come to mind.

The stones that pass through the body, leaving the body unchanged.

The stones that must be shattered: they are broken, the body is left unchanged. The stones that must be surgically treated: the body is opened, they leave unchanged.

The mass inside you that resists encouragement, that refuses the slip of the spontaneous passage.

Sometimes obstinacy manifests as inertia, which is an apparently neutral position. It feels as if your body has not caught up to the world; it feels as if the world has not caught up to your body.

Disinclination comes up against the fear of not being missed.

6

> There are things that would delete
> themselves if only you would let them, damage
>
> to the circulation, and that is what I wanted.
> Was a gasped voice from the beginning,
>
> overly phlegmatic, striated to perfection,
> the colour of our facets and we wouldn't be
>
> blind. And I could hold myself within me
> so tight that I might burst; prolapse of the
>
> epidermis – is that you, polymorphous pervert,
> moaning, ah, fuck me in the plural. (Uziell 2016: 4)

7

There are bodies that would dissolve, that would not be contingent upon the argument of their embodiment. There are arguments that would admit points to the point of atrophy.

In moving round desires, we go from death to death: 'But the advantage of syncope is precisely that one always returns from it. Asthmatics, epileptics, lovers – they recount explicitly how wonderful it is to breathe after the attack. [...] We place ourselves in the *before* death, in the *after* death. The real crossing is forgotten' (Clément 1994: 15). The inability to speak precedes asphyxiation; there is no question apart from the question of who comes first.

The destroyer of strength said: 'It is built up with bones, smeared over with flesh, covered with skin, filled with faeces, urine, bile, phlegm, marrow, fat, grease and also with many diseases, like a treasure house full of wealth' (Radhakrishnan 1989: 807). I am full of fullness.

The destroyer of strength said: 'In such a world as this, what is the good of the enjoyment of desires?' (797). My eyes are full of fullness.

Over-identifying with you, I am unable to speak or listen or respond to you. Compressed by the fullness of bodies, my body implodes. (Inertia may manifest as love.)

The argument is hypertrophic, admitting too many colours and consistencies. My desires are irreducible to the point.

8

बिंदु **bindu,** a detached particle, drop, globule; a pearl; a drop of water taken as a measure; a spot or mark of coloured paint on the body of an elephant; the dot over a letter representing the *anusvāra* [after-sound] (supposed to be connected with Śiva and of great mystical importance);

a zero or cypher (in manuscripts put over an erased word to show that it ought not to be erased); a mark made by the teeth of a lover on the lips

9

Orgasm is therefore the foremost means of attaining the dissolution of the individual subject, who thereby becomes the Absolute I, the Immense Heart, or a Forbidden Word. This notion of favouring the moment of syncope is pushed to its extreme consequences; it is true that afterward nothing of value remains. Not sex, nor death, incest, excrement, urine, or even God: it's all the same, or rather, it's All One. (Clément 1994: 139)

10

I light fires in your stomach to worship the tiger eye in your eyes.

The body becomes rancid in the warmth of the embrace.

I absorb your inability, in me the juncture is hardened in fire.

I absorb your inability, in me the hardness reaches extinction.

I absorb the world between you and us, in me the white world reaches extinction.

The body comes into the world, continues into the world, dissolves into the world.

'Thereafter it burns the world, devoid of lustre, devoid of limit, devoid of appearance. It burns the *mahat tattva*: it burns the Unmanifested. It burns the Imperishable. It burns Death' (Radhakrishnan 1989: 890).

In the deadness of night, our eyes filled with slime –

Tell us the great secret of aloneness –

Likeness to likeness, we are utterly fucked.

Bibliography

Ahmed, Sara, *On Being Included: Racism and Diversity in Institutional Life* (Durham: Duke University Press, 2012)

Clément, Catherine, *Syncope: The Philosophy of Rapture*, trans. by Sally O'Driscoll and Deirdre M. Mahoney (Minneapolis: University of Minnesota, 1994)

Fanon, Frantz, *Black Skin, White Masks*, trans. by Charles Lam Markmann (London: Pluto Press, 2008)

Monier-Williams, Monier, *A Sanskrit-English Dictionary: Etymologically and Philologically Arranged with Special Reference to Cognate Indo-European Languages* (New Delhi: Asian Educational Services, 2008)

OED Online (Oxford University Press, 2016)

Radhakrishnan, S., ed., *The Principal Upaniṣads* (New Delhi: Oxford University Press, 1989)

Uziell, Lawrence, 'untitled', *ZARF*, No. 3 (Spring 2016), p. 4

Michael Symmons Roberts

In Paradisum

Three thousand refugee children arrive in our city,
or rather, camp on flood-plains by the ship canal,
or rather, have no tents, so sit down
among thistles and dock and nettles,
on rain-hammered concrete,
hang their backpacks on spars of rusted iron
up from the earth like ribs of giants disinterred.
Soon they make a tarpaulin village.

Unaccompanied, three thousand refugee children
are leaderless, and though we dare not think
of what they hold inside their heads
they look for all the world like any kids
with their ball-games and fights and gangs.
Not that we know how three thousand refugee children
should behave, but we will know when we see it.
We slow our cars past them as a mark of respect,

and three thousand refugee children
return that nobility by looking back at us,
as if in a slow-motion tracking shot at the end
of a film when the train sets off to rescue or deport,
and some are aboard but some are not. Trust us,
we will determine what three thousand refugee children
need and give it to them. Our best minds are on it,
and will not sleep until the strategy is clear.

In the meantime, we have to go to work.
We have to tend to the numbers, to ensure
we keep unrestricted funds from restricted funds,
unprotected assets from protected assets.

We have to maintain the beauty of our public spaces,
to live as fully as we can in the present moment,
because that is what three thousand refugee children
long for, and to lose it is to let them down.

Believe us, we have tried to find interpreters,
but three thousand refugee children speak
a dialect of a dialect of a long-lost tongue
beyond the ears of our philologists.
Some nights, we leave a window open
to listen for the cries of three thousand refugee children,
in the hope that a cry might unlock it for us,
or unlock something inside us.

Other nights we lie awake and try to separate
them in our minds, to give them names,
so the one in the Brazil shirt becomes *Paulo*,
and the one in the blue smock his cousin *Lily*,
and their parents worked a dry field in the hills,
and their grandparents repaired shoes
and kept an unwritten repository of stories
to pass on to three thousand refugee children.

And their days in the homeland, though spare,
though lean, were on the whole benign
until those flares on the horizon grew closer,
and closer, and came for them.
But no sooner, in the ease of night, have we
begun to picture them, than some fox in a bin
breaks the trance and *Lily* and *Paulo* snap back
into three thousand refugee children.

James Sheard

November

Let me tell you how, in this long dark,
I list the ways in which the leaf of you
unfurled and furled around me.

It is a thought like woodsmoke
entering the blood – the chambers
of the heart can only clutch at it.

Penelope Shuttle

Doreen Shows Me Her Photos of Hamelin

It was the total lack
of hospitality at Hamelin
that pissed-off the Piper,

all his music, gratis,
plus the rat exodus,
but not a sip of beer,

not a peck of soup,
a town about as friendly
as a childless house.

So be it.
The last child into the mountain
looks back, smiling.

In Doreen's crowded attic
there's a stone rat she souvenired
during her ATS days in Occupied Germany,

she'd like to return it to the tableau
at Hamelin,
with apologies,

but it is much too bulky for her to transport,
at her age.
Over tea, we decide no one will miss

a single stone rat,
not after all these years,
not now that Europe is one big happy family.

Safiya Sinclair

Hymen Elegy

Disobeyed. Sucked the blooded marrow dark, unhooded
    its martyr, wildflower effusing with such
headless agency. Stripped blind my one eye, mutable as the dream

before a storm. Cursed the sterile sky. Cursed the rapeseed
    that fathered you, unfathered me, cursed myself.
Appraised as a trinket, I gave a cowrie shell away. Sold

first to the adulterer, then hawked to shoeless Adam, peddled
    to schoolboys on the country bus. Scratched the demigod
who stole it, dressed as a Judas steer, red moon bellowing.
    Hot nostril-steam

down my back. Dammed my wet scream around those verbs
    for a violence. But I am all teeth. I did not snitch. Went braless
like a bad bitch, horned slick, turned sacral, crotched gold
    in my wife-

beater and asked for it. Bless my vanity. My charity. How like
    a parted urchin she fills and fills with rheum. Made a killing,
like our language, of the woman I had pilloried. *What a sight*

prized the white man pushing his Mag-Lite into it, a game to see
    just where a girl like me could go. *So tight* he whispered
from beyond the haze, thrusting until she was no longer a part of me,

undone under world, pressed full and unfathomed, pulped raw
    as a meathole. O plastic. O raggedy-ann. This is what you wanted.
Ripped button for eyes and yarn for hair; she will not grow nor come

alive. How widening loneliness is a gift again. First opening
   greedy on that Christmas bulb, flush, lit-up. Half-angel.
The old ghost, unfondling on his tender threat, will never
   knock me up.

Karen Solie

An Enthusiast

Endless heritage beneath the heavenly soundshed.
Jet-black amphiboles. Ten varieties of scones
in Elie. Giant centipedes and petrified tree stumps of the Devonian
fossil record. Pyrope garnets at the foot

of the Lady's Tower aren't quite rare enough
to acquire significant market value, much like the self-taught experts
in autobrecciation and exfoliation weathering
who work their way to the surface of the Coastal Path

at the close of a hard winter. Amateur
geologists, rockhounds, and collectors may be distinguished
by commitments to task-specific outerwear,
but a bin bag rain poncho is not the measure of a person.

Ideas gather around phenomena as though for warmth.
Between art and science, our method is the stage
upon which the universal plays in the fragment. Form in
number, ratio in form. A nice bit of white-trap,

or ironstone in a setting of green tuff
inspire a loyalty appropriate to no other relationship.
In the floodlights of taxonomy subjects
evaporate, at peace, and an uncompromised image steps forward.

I like it at sea level. It's the right amount of exposition for me,
on the shores of the Great Archive. When you bring pain,
as you feel you must, when the exhausting singularity
spreads through my limbs, I look to sandstone

understanding itself by breaking at joints produced by the forces.
To the stacks preferentially and justly eroded
along their planes of weakness when seas
were four metres higher. As again they well may be.

George Szirtes

The Yellow Room *an extract*

1

Late father, you mystery, father of diminishing returns,
how do you weigh in the scale now, by what measure should I
examine you, when you are literally dust, which is nothing
but dust, not a meaning that might any day cohere
into the complex singularity that was addressed by name.

There should, I feel, be something solid about a name,
something gathered and whole, something that brought us here
as if by appointment, that had not arisen out of nothing
but out of name itself, the point at which you become an I
and to which the whole that is gathered eventually returns.

2

Once there was a room which was, like any other room,
fit to be born into or to stare out from, a room half-darkness,
half unquenchable light. Someone might lie down in it
or sit at a table, engaged in the act of doing and thinking,
inhabiting the room into which you as a self were born.

Let me imagine that moment, the instant of being born,
carried into a world that is not particularly thinking
of your particular moment, unconcerned with your place in it.
Time starts collapsing: it vanishes into the musty darkness
it waits in and fills up every secret corner of the room.

3

Chairs and sofas and pictures and sideboards and mornings. The door
is open. The noise of the morning is wheels, bells and cries.
The street is the one street. The house, one among many
closed universes, rushes backwards in time as you thrust forward.
You have arrived just in time, just as time was closing,
closing and collapsing, just as the door itself was closing.

There never will be another opportunity to look forward
to this. It is at this point that you become the many.
I am trying to distinguish your cry from all those other cries,
but all there is is the door, which is by now a closed door.

4
I understand nothing.
                    I have followed no trail.

When leaves move against the wall, it is no language.

    When sun strikes the leaves it is an exclamation without sound.

I overhear   it is all incompletion,   the tongues of leaves   the open
    mouths of flowers.

Things happen. They stand in rows. They form orderly queues.
    They are hungry.

I cannot begin to unpick the clues without language. I need to
    understand
                    what a clue is   what language is.

These lines are blown across the page as in a gust.

        I must order them.

5
These stanzas are closed rooms closing on themselves
with stiff internal doors. I enter, stirring a draught,
raising the corners of newspapers, and the reader
rises, or raises an eyebrow, briefly to register
an entrance, then returns to the fascinating article

he was reading, himself becoming an article
in the space provided, and I am not sure how to register
his presence, or yours, my patient, magnificent reader.

The doors of our meeting seem to permit of a draught.
Closed doors must have been opening themselves.

Laura Watson

Chickens

Speaking of conditioned behavior in a cold Florida classroom,
our teacher, who seemed always to have just finished a cigarette

and whose perfectly dentured mouth said *fangers* and *warsh*,
took, by way of example, the yardstick

from its dusty cradle that hung below the chalkboard,
and brought it, full force, flat side against the lectern.

The resulting *thwack* – pure, parochial – carried through the class.
It hit off the concrete block and the waxed tile floor,

off the air-conditioned tops of the science tables
where, the week before, a line of frogs

was pinned in flight before us. And more to his point,
it travelled over us, through us, our twelve year-old selves,

to the back of the lab, where it fell over the brood
of yellow-brown chicks warming themselves under the heat lamps

and pecking at the shit-upon newspaper that lined their temporary
    pen.
Each, and all at once, their soft bodies went still,

except in their stillness there was something
that made them sway: forward, backward, forward again

in a short, invisible arc, each a little pendulum
counting the time, until, one by one, the full dozen of them

recovered. Caroline, as willowy as her mother,
will find her stepfather in bed beside her. She snapped upright

in her chair, the heavy yellow curls of her hair
swinging to and fro in the inch above her shoulders.

Thwack. Heidi, at twenty-five, will violate
parole. She sat apart, in the first row, the first to see the yardstick

raised in the air, and the first to feel it move
a thin bar of air in front of her. She leaned into it –

the breeze and the backswing – before softening
in her chair. *Thwack*. Our teacher swung the yardstick

a fourth time, a fifth, the worn white oak of the lectern
giving up to the fluorescent air a veil of chalk dust,

almost a comet's tail, that split the room in two,
and as it settled, the chicks behind us paused and swayed

and began again their small activity. *Thwack*. Jessie,
in her quiet way, will swallow all the aspirin

she can find. *Thwack*. Brad will lose his brother. Jason, his dad.
Two of us will go to war and one of us will come back.

Thwack. The sun filtered through the chicken-wire windows
casting a wattled shadow on the opposite wall

and we sat in the full light of the classroom. *Thwack*.
And the chickens, by then, there was no pause in them at all.

Chrissy Williams

Bear of the Artist

I asked the artist to draw me a heart and instead he drew a bear.

I asked him, 'What kind of heart is this?' and he said, 'It's not a
heart at all.'

I asked him, 'What kind of bear is this?' and he said, 'It's not a
bear either.'

I asked him, 'What kind of artist are you anyway?' and he said,

'I am the one who exists to put bears in your head, who exists

to put ideas in your head in place of bears, who mistrusts anyone

who tells you they know what kind of place the heart is, the head,

how it should look, what size, what stopping distances, etc.,

and as long as you keep me existing to put bears in your head

I will, because nights are getting darker, and we're all tired,

we're all so tired, and everyone could use a bear sometimes,

everyone could use a wild bear, though they can be dangerous

and there's nothing worse than a bear in the face, when it breaks –

always remember how your bear breaks down

against the shore, the shore, the shore.'

Alex Wong

Embellishment

On a hot particular day
When the loose, broad spread of an iris,
    Blue, faint as a vein,

Like a long-time missed initial   in fancy majuscule,—
    Seemed, in generous lapse
        of limb, poised slack and easy,
Equal expression for all things of that day,—

This deeper blue,—reflex,
        faced fair in the shallow pool,—
Still wet, when we pass,
In the road, where the wagtail

      Bent,
      sharp,
      at the border
      to drink,—

Was asking to be furled in my rocaille;—
    Though I am on better terms with the frilled iris:
It is erotic; I know what to do with it.

Karen McCarthy Woolf

& Because

a string of unilluminated dragonflies dangles
from the ceiling

our screens glow
like fireflies
at opposite ends of the flat, one of us
facing south, the other
north,

the anglepoise reflected
like a moon in the cracked glass— yes,
it's cracked but it endures,
the empty spaces I crave are filled
with dust
dating back to the nineteenth century

& because I can't forget
the torrent
of the m6 as we switched
lanes on the way back from the retrospective
where we took
photos of you standing by a painting
of your mother in 1975,
how she stared
out of a window, determined
not to smile
and of course your hair is the colour of her hair,
and the gallery walls are white

& because roses aren't what they used to be, so few
are fragrant and only a fraction
of those that survive the shivery hold
unfurl into fullness,
their thorns
bred out like pips from a watermelon

&
because water is no longer sacred, our rivers
run like sores
and mountain streams are bottled, sold,
binned then spun
into the gyres of the Pacific

Biographies of the shortlisted writers

Forward Prize for Best Collection

Nuar Alsadir (b. Connecticut, USA) works as a psychotherapist, psychoanalyst and academic in New York. 'The mind doesn't see images, hear, smell, perceive in tidy succession,' she says. 'That cacophonous chaos, which visual arts often capture so vividly, is exciting to me.'

Alsadir, born of Iraqi parents, responded strongly to coverage of the Iraq war. 'I began to realize the extent to which the chaos of the external world – and my internal world – demanded accurate expression. More than ever, the ready-made forms did not feel relevant to me or able to truthfully hold what the world – or I – had become.' *Fourth Person Singular* is a deeply politically engaged book, which dares its readers into new ways of ordering their thoughts and the information around them.

Tara Bergin (b. 1974 Dublin) writes that 'traditional songs…appeal to me a great deal and they have influenced much of my writing'.

In *The Tragic Death of Eleanor Marx*, Bergin plays with various narratives, most notably those recounting the deaths of Eleanor Marx (daughter of Karl) and of Flaubert's Emma Bovary. These poems are intellectually complex – a deep commentary on the politics of gender and family – while remaining songlike and, as she writes, 'enjoyable to listen to'.

In 2012 Bergin completed a PhD on Ted Hughes's translations of János Pilinszky, and now lives in Yorkshire. She is interested in 'changes that happen to English when it is spoken by non-English voices', and in the relationship between her native Ireland and other countries.

Emily Berry (b. 1981 London), editor of *The Poetry Review*, is shortlisted for her second book, *Stranger, Baby*. It addresses, she says, 'the long shadow cast by the loss of a mother in childhood – my own loss'.

Her first, *Dear Boy*, won the Forward Prize for Best First Collection in 2013. That book focused on eerie, elliptical narratives and askance, lively interactions with the discourse around mental health, gender, domestic (dis)harmony and psychoanalysis.

Stranger, Baby develops these approaches in a more personally intimate space. 'There are,' she says, 'a lot of other people's words in the book alongside my own. So it's lonely but it's also companionable.'

Michael Longley (b. 1939 Belfast) wrote his first poem over 60 years ago, at the age of 16, 'in order to impress a girlfriend'. His poetry has continued to impress widely: his honours include the Whitbread Poetry Award, the Hawthornden Prize, the TS Eliot Prize, the Queen's Gold Medal for Poetry and, most recently, the PEN Pinter Prize. His friend, the late Seamus Heaney, described him as 'a custodian of griefs and wonders'.

Longley, who cites the work of Edward Thomas and WB Yeats as touchstones, demonstrates in *Angel Hill* a luminous and engaged sparseness of style. He says, 'My work has become simpler as I have grown older…writing a poem is a journey into the unknown. Poetry is a mystery.' Invested in nature and morality, *Angel Hill* finds a beautiful ground for that mystery.

Sinéad Morrissey (b. 1972 Portadown) was Belfast's inaugural Poet Laureate until 2016, and is now professor of creative writing at the University of Newcastle. She has published six collections, including the 2013 TS Eliot Prize-winning book *Parallax*.

Morrissey describes *On Balance* as her 'most cohesive book' to date. 'Just as it says on the tin, the book interrogates ideas of balance – physical balance, structural balance, gender balance, ecological balance, life-death balance – and it does so using the high-wire act of poetic form as a conduit for that exploration.'

Combining a subtlety of touch with a powerful turn of phrase – one character finds in all things 'the über-florid signature of God' – Morrissey manages to hold narrative and lyric in delicate relation.

Felix Dennis Prize for Best First Collection

Maria Apichella (b. 1985 Oxford) completed her PhD at the University of Aberystwyth, combining study with several jobs. 'Every aspect of life feeds into writing: from teaching to cleaning toilets, to working in a call centre by night to sitting in the Welsh National Library reading Dylan Thomas on rainy afternoons.'

Apichella won the Melita Hume Poetry Prize for the manuscript which became *Psalmody*. 'I used Psalm-like rhythms, metaphors and images, gaining inspiration from the human body, food and place.' *Psalmody* is also vividly worldly and contemporary in its depiction of the relationship between the religious speaker and her atheist partner: 'I love to argue back, / Celtic talker, poet-mouth; you'll never stop exploring, / taking everything apart like a nerd.'

Richard Georges (b. 1982 Port of Spain, Trinidad) was raised and now lives in the British Virgin Islands. As an undergraduate he found himself 'falling in love with images and rhyme and would find parallels between writers like Walcott and Eliot with lyrical rappers like Nas and Eminem'.

Make Us All Islands is various, familiar and challenging by turns, but keeps returning to what Georges describes as its 'bones'. 'Those bones speak to certain submerged narratives of the British Virgin Islands, a place which is rich in histories that aren't well understood here, and almost unknown abroad. *Make Us All Islands* attempts to write those narratives into the Caribbean landscape, to fill these island-sized gaps.'

Eric Langley (b. 1977 Birmingham) lectures in Shakespeare and Renaissance literature at UCL. He turned to writing poetry in 2011, after the death of his father – award-winning poet RF Langley. 'When the real poet of the family died, I found that writing poetry was a way of continuing conversations which we'd had.'

He is fascinated by 'connections between people (eyebeams, communication, arrows, interactions traversing the interim between people, verbal and emotional transmissions)'. *Raking Light* manages to be simultaneously riotous and high-minded, metaphysical and modern, austere and romantic. 'I take my cue from the art restoration technique of "raking light", when a beam is shone across the picture plane to reveal over-painting, under-drawing, the artist's first intentions, buried depths: *pentimenti*, or regrets.'

Nick Makoha (b. 1974 Lumino, Uganda) fled Uganda's civil war and Idi Amin's tyranny as a boy. The childhood hobby of poetry gave way to a sense of vocation when he completed a degree in biochemistry in the UK. On daring to quit his London nine-to-five banking job, he set fire to his suits. 'I did this to remind me that I did not want an easy way back. I wanted to give my all to the art of writing.'

The poet Kwame Dawes, teaching at Arvon, first made him feel like a poet. 'He asked me, "What type of poet do you want to be; one that obscures or one that reveals?" Till then I felt like I was treading water but after that conversation I was aware of a burning purpose forming inside of me.' That purpose is manifest in *Kingdom of Gravity*, a searing but mysterious contemplation of exile, fatherhood and violence.

Ocean Vuong (b. 1988 outside Saigon, Vietnam) was the first member of his immediate family to be able to read or write but has been around the oral tradition of poetry since birth. A refugee, he moved to the US at the age of two. He lives in New York, and studied with Ben Lerner at Brooklyn College.

In its powerful contemplations of brutality, family and sexuality, *Night Sky with Exit Wounds* is throughout almost religious and almost profane. This is poetry of questions which refuses to separate the intensely personal from the globally political. It's also an investigation into writing. Vuong says he is 'interested in that shifting of meaning and usage because it feels innately Queer to me – how language, like people, can be perpetually in flux'. Words, he says, 'are, in a sense, bodies moving from one space to another'.

Forward Prize for Best Single Poem

Malika Booker (b. 1970 London) is the author of *Breadfruit*, a Poetry Book Society Recommendation, and *Pepper Seed*. She was the inaugural poet-in-residence at the Royal Shakespeare Company and a Fellow of both Cave Canem and The Complete Works. She also appears alongside Sharon Olds and Warsan Shire in *Penguin Modern Poets 3*.

Booker is of Guyanese and Grenadian parentage, and 'Nine Nights' is taken from a series of poems around Caribbean funerals. The poem takes the form of nine fragments, and charts a vivid intersection between biblical and Grenadian funeral rites. 'Lazarus dash way hymns and cuss words from he house with the heavy bass of a thumping speaker box.'

Mary Jean Chan (b. 1990 Hong Kong) has been a Fellow of Callaloo and VONA, and is currently a research associate at the Royal Holloway Poetics Research Centre at the University of London.

She says her poem '//' was 'born out of an intensely personal experience, and also informed by ruminations on the state of mental health amongst LGBTQ youths in a city that I flee from, yet constantly wish to return to'. Its rolling couplets manage the trick of being simultaneously intimate, passionate and politically widely-scoped: 'How many / times have you and I wondered about leaving our bodies / behind, the way many of us have already left?'

Harmony Holiday (b. 1982 Iowa, USA) is the author of books including *Negro League Baseball, Go Find Your Father/A Famous Blues* and *Hollywood Forever*.

As the daughter of musician Jimmy Holiday, she was immersed in music from early childhood: 'I just thought it was part of being human, to communicate in some form of sound grammar outside of the mundane daily rhythms and speech patterns. I never really separated poetry from music and music from the body and dance, from ways of moving through space and time.'

'The City Admits no Wrongdoing' is built around Billie Holiday, as a singer, an icon and a subject of 'poised suffering'. Written without line-breaks, it finds its urgent rhythm in the patterns of unexpected connections: 'She loved candies. We need sugar. We run on sugar. Melanin is carbon. Carbon is sugar. Billie is shook, hurry, you love her.'

Ishion Hutchinson (b. 1983 Port Antonio, Jamaica) teaches on the graduate writing programme at Cornell University. His poetry collections include *Far District* and *House of Lords and Commons*. He first felt himself to be a poet early in childhood; it became a vocation followed in high school. 'The rest is devotion and luck.' That luck includes the right teachers and the right books, though he also credits the growth of his imagination to his Jamaican background, particularly 'its elemental power as much as the force of its historical current'.

'Nightfall, Jane Ash Corner, St. Thomas' also seeks to overlay landscape with history and the movements of culture: 'Progress is back, but centuries / are one here.' The poem handles its materials delicately, allowing them to remain both symbolic and sensual. 'The first solid draft,' he writes, 'came last year after I read a poem called "That Place", by RS Thomas, and something blistering and striking in the words "To return to after the bitter / Migrations," jolted me towards my poem.'

Ian Patterson (b. 1948 Birmingham) has taught English for almost 20 years at Queens' College, Cambridge. His academic books include *Guernica and Total War*. He's published numerous works of poetry, including, more recently, *Time to Get Here: Selected Poems 1969-2002*, *Still Life* and *Bound To Be*.

Patterson's poetry comes from 'an awareness that poems were a strange form of knowledge with the capacity to arouse intuitive or unconscious responses, almost like echoes of being'. 'The Plenty of Nothing' is an elegy to his late wife, the writer Jenny Diski. It's a moving, unsettled and capacious poem, enacting the attempt to 'get enough pink forms to reconcile / two worlds of the mind', 'two / true stories in matters'. The poem depicts a struggle, in the face of mortality and of – in Wallace Stevens' words – the 'Nothing that is not there and the nothing that is'.

Publisher acknowledgements

Rachael Allen · Many Bird Roast · *Poetry London*

Nuar Alsadir · Sketch 19 · Sketch 64 · *Fourth Person Singular* ·
Pavilion Poetry

Maria Apichella · 28 · 58 · *Psalmody* · Eyewear Publishing

Simon Armitage · I Kicked a Mushroom · *The Unaccompanied* ·
Faber & Faber

Tara Bergin · The True Story of Eleanor Marx · The True Story
of Eleanor Marx in Ten Parts · *The Tragic Death of Eleanor Marx* ·
Carcanet

Emily Berry · Winter · Aura · *Stranger, Baby* · Faber & Faber

Rachael Boast · Coda: Lost Poem · *Void Studies* · Picador Poetry

Malika Booker · Nine Nights · *The Poetry Review*

Andrea Brady · Salthouse · *The Strong Room* · Crater 42

Alan Buckley · Scum · *The Morning Star*

Elizabeth-Jane Burnett · *from* Swims · *Swims* · Penned in the Margins

John Burnside · The Lazarus Taxa · *Still Life with Feeding Snake* ·
Cape Poetry

Michelle Cahill · The End of the Dream · *The Herring Lass* ·
Arc Publications

Vahni Capildeo · Blood · *Poetry London*

Mary Jean Chan · // · *Ambit*

Becky Cherriman · Jesus Lives · *Empires of Clay* · Cinnamon Press

Kayo Chingonyi · Alternate Take · *Kumukanda* · Chatto & Windus

Theodoros Chiotis · Interference (or, Uncommon Time for the
Medicalised Subject) · Litmus Publishing

Maya Chowdhry · Butterfly Orchid · *Fossil* · Peepal Tree

Elisabeth Sennitt Clough · Boy · *Sightings* · Pindrop Press

Kelvin Corcoran · At the Hospital Doors · *Facing West* ·
Shearsman Books

Keki Daruwalla · In night country · *Acumen*

Rishi Dastidar · What's the matter with [insert (non-metropolitan)
English constituency of choice]? · *Ticker-tape* · Nine Arches Press

US Dhuga · Philoctetes at the Gym · *The Sight Of A Goose Going Barefoot* ·
Eyewear Poetry

Douglas Dunn · Class Photograph · *The Noise of a Fly* · Faber & Faber

Steve Ely · Jerusalem · *Incendium Amoris* · Smokestack Books
John Foggin · A Weak Force · *Much Possessed* · Smith|Doorstop
Miriam Gamble · The Oak That Was Not There · *Poetry Ireland Review*
Richard Georges · Ghazal of Guyana · Oceans · *Make Us All Islands* ·
    Shearsman Books
Philip Gross · Back · *New Welsh Review*
Harmony Holiday · The City Admits no Wrongdoing · *Prac Crit*
Jodie Hollander · Dream of a Burning Woman · *My Dark Horses* ·
    Pavilion Poetry
Wayne Holloway-Smith · Some Waynes · *Alarum* · Bloodaxe Books
Ishion Hutchinson · Nightfall, Jane Ash Corner, St. Thomas ·
    The Well Review
Rosalind Jana · Hollow · *Branch and Vein* · New River Press
Zaffar Kunial · Prayer · *The Poetry Review*
Eric Langley · 1. Of those from the ships · Pentimenti · *Raking Light* ·
    Carcanet
Michael Longley · Angel Hill · Room to Rhyme · *Angel Hill* ·
    Cape Poetry
Nick Makoha · Prayers for Exiled Poets · At Gunpoint · *Kingdom of
    Gravity* · Peepal Tree
Shara McCallum · Vesta to Madwoman · *Madwoman* · Peepal Tree
Niall McDevitt · Lithostrotos · *Firing Slits: Jerusalem Colportage* ·
    New River Press
Momtaza Mehri · Portrait Of An Intimate Terrorist In His Natural
    Habitat · *The Rialto*
Jessica Mookherjee · Ursa Minor · *The Journal*
Sinéad Morrissey · Perfume · My Life According to You · *On Balance* ·
    Carcanet
Paul Muldoon · Walnuts · *Poetry Ireland Review*
André Naffis-Sahely · Postcard from the Cape · *The Promised Land* ·
    Penguin Books
Daljit Nagra · Father of Only Daughters · *British Museum* ·
    Faber & Faber
Miriam Nash · The Father's Caesarean · *All the Prayers in the House* ·
    Bloodaxe Books
Charlotte Newman · All that Jazz · *Trammel* · Penned in the Margins
Sean O'Brien · One Way or Another · *Times Literary Supplement*

Ian Patterson · The Plenty of Nothing · *PN Review*

Pascale Petit · Mama Amazonica · *Mama Amazonica* · Bloodaxe Books

Jacob Polley · Every Creeping Thing · *Jackself* · Picador Poetry

Nisha Ramayya · Secretions or Obstructions · Litmus Publishing

Michael Symmons Roberts · In Paradisum · *Mancunia* · Cape Poetry

James Sheard · November · *The Abandoned Settlements* · Cape Poetry

Penelope Shuttle · Doreen Shows Me Her Photos of Hamelin ·
   ARTEMISpoetry

Safiya Sinclair · Hymen Elegy · *Granta*

Karen Solie · An Enthusiast · *London Review of Books*

George Szirtes · The Yellow Room · *Mapping the Delta* · Bloodaxe Books

Ocean Vuong · Telemachus · Notebook Fragments · *Night Sky with Exit
   Wounds* · Cape Poetry

Laura Watson · Chickens · Bridport Prize

Chrissy Williams · Bear of the Artist · *Bear* · Bloodaxe Books

Alex Wong · Embellishment · *Poems without Irony* · Carcanet

Karen McCarthy Woolf · & Because · *Seasonal Disturbances* · Carcanet

Winners of the Forward Prizes

Best Collection

2016 · Vahni Capildeo · *Measures of Expatriation* · Carcanet

2015 · Claudia Rankine · *Citizen: An American Lyric* · Penguin Books

2014 · Kei Miller · *The Cartographer Tries to Map a Way to Zion* · Carcanet

2013 · Michael Symmons Roberts · *Drysalter* · Cape Poetry

2012 · Jorie Graham · *PLACE* · Carcanet

2011 · John Burnside · *Black Cat Bone* · Cape Poetry

2010 · Seamus Heaney · *Human Chain* · Faber & Faber

2009 · Don Paterson · *Rain* · Faber & Faber

2008 · Mick Imlah · *The Lost Leader* · Faber & Faber

2007 · Sean O'Brien · *The Drowned Book* · Picador Poetry

2006 · Robin Robertson · *Swithering* · Picador Poetry

2005 · David Harsent · *Legion* · Faber & Faber

2004 · Kathleen Jamie · *The Tree House* · Picador Poetry

2003 · Ciaran Carson · *Breaking News* · The Gallery Press

2002 · Peter Porter · *Max is Missing* · Picador Poetry

2001 · Sean O'Brien · *Downriver* · Picador Poetry

2000 · Michael Donaghy · *Conjure* · Picador Poetry

1999 · Jo Shapcott · *My Life Asleep* · OUP

1998 · Ted Hughes · *Birthday Letters* · Faber & Faber

1997 · Jamie McKendrick · *The Marble Fly* · OUP

1996 · John Fuller · *Stones and Fires* · Chatto & Windus

1995 · Sean O'Brien · *Ghost Train* · OUP

1994 · Alan Jenkins · *Harm* · Chatto & Windus

1993 · Carol Ann Duffy · *Mean Time* · Anvil Press

1992 · Thom Gunn · *The Man with Night Sweats* · Faber & Faber

Best First Collection

2016 · Tiphanie Yanique · *Wife* · Peepal Tree

2015 · Mona Arshi · *Small Hands* · Pavilion Poetry

2014 · Liz Berry · *Black Country* · Chatto & Windus

2013 · Emily Berry · *Dear Boy* · Faber & Faber

2012 · Sam Riviere · *81 Austerities* · Faber & Faber

2011 · Rachael Boast · *Sidereal* · Picador Poetry

2010 · Hilary Menos · *Berg* · Seren

2009 · Emma Jones · *The Striped World* · Faber & Faber
2008 · Kathryn Simmonds · *Sunday at the Skin Launderette* · Seren
2007 · Daljit Nagra · *Look We Have Coming to Dover!* · Faber & Faber
2006 · Tishani Doshi · *Countries of the Body* · Aark Arts
2005 · Helen Farish · *Intimates* · Cape Poetry
2004 · Leontia Flynn · *These Days* · Cape Poetry
2003 · AB Jackson · *Fire Stations* · Anvil Press
2002 · Tom French · *Touching the Bones* · The Gallery Press
2001 · John Stammers · *Panoramic Lounge-Bar* · Picador Poetry
2000 · Andrew Waterhouse · *In* · The Rialto
1999 · Nick Drake · *The Man in the White Suit* · Bloodaxe Books
1998 · Paul Farley · *The Boy from the Chemist is Here to See You* ·
        Picador Poetry
1997 · Robin Robertson · *A Painted Field* · Picador Poetry
1996 · Kate Clanchy · *Slattern* · Chatto & Windus
1995 · Jane Duran · *Breathe Now, Breathe* · Enitharmon
1994 · Kwame Dawes · *Progeny of Air* · Peepal Tree
1993 · Don Paterson · *Nil Nil* · Faber & Faber
1992 · Simon Armitage · *Kid* · Faber & Faber

Best Single Poem
2016 · Sasha Dugdale · Joy · *PN Review*
2015 · Claire Harman · The Mighty Hudson · *Times Literary Supplement*
2014 · Stephen Santus · In a Restaurant · Bridport Prize
2013 · Nick MacKinnon · The Metric System · *The Warwick Review*
2012 · Denise Riley · A Part Song · *London Review of Books*
2011 · RF Langley · To a Nightingale · *London Review of Books*
2010 · Julia Copus · An Easy Passage · *Magma*
2009 · Robin Robertson · At Roane Head · *London Review of Books*
2008 · Don Paterson · Love Poem for Natalie "Tusja" Beridze ·
        The Poetry Review
2007 · Alice Oswald · Dunt · *Poetry London*
2006 · Sean O'Brien · Fantasia on a Theme of James Wright ·
        The Poetry Review
2005 · Paul Farley · Liverpool Disappears for a Billionth of a Second ·
        The North

2004 · Daljit Nagra · Look We Have Coming to Dover! ·
The Poetry Review

2003 · Robert Minhinnick · The Fox in the Museum of Wales ·
Poetry London

2002 · Medbh McGuckian · She Is in the Past, She Has This Grace ·
The Shop

2001 · Ian Duhig · The Lammas Hireling · National Poetry Competition

2000 · Tessa Biddington · The Death of Descartes · Bridport Prize

1999 · Robert Minhinnick · Twenty-five Laments for Iraq · *PN Review*

1998 · Sheenagh Pugh · Envying Owen Beattie · *New Welsh Review*

1997 · Lavinia Greenlaw · A World Where News Travelled Slowly · *Times Literary Supplement*

1996 · Kathleen Jamie · The Graduates · *Times Literary Supplement*

1995 · Jenny Joseph · In Honour of Love · *The Rialto*

1994 · Iain Crichton Smith · Autumn · *PN Review*

1993 · Vicki Feaver · Judith · *Independent on Sunday*

1992 · Jackie Kay · Black Bottom · Bloodaxe Books

For more detail and further reading about the Forward Prizes, books and associated programmes, see our website forwardartsfoundation.org or follow us on Facebook or Twitter @ForwardPrizes